Reading Through History

Oklahoma History:

Early History Through Statehood

By Jake Henderson & Robert Marshall

Oklahoma History
Early History Through Statehood
by Jake Henderson & Robert Marshall
©2015

ISBN-13: 978-1508530374
ISBN-10: 1508530378

Please visit our sites at
https://www.facebook.com/ReadingThroughHistory
http://readingthroughhistory.com

Table of Contents:

(Continued on the next page)

Earliest Native Settlers

Native Americans have lived in Oklahoma for thousands of years. Which native tribes lived in the area? What were their lives like?

The earliest natives to live in Oklahoma were nomadic wanderers. These tribes hunted big-game animals such as the wooly mammoth. The oldest settlements found in the state belong to the Clovis people. The tribe was given this name because evidence of their existence was first discovered near Clovis, New Mexico. The Clovis people lived in Oklahoma approximately 8,000 to 12,000 years ago.

Archaeologists have found considerable evidence of the Clovis people's presence, as well as that of other ancient native tribes. Spear points, tar-lined bags (for carrying water), and mammoth skulls with painted markings have all been discovered. They have also found multiple sites where mammoth were tracked down and killed at that location.

About 7,000 years ago, bands of foragers moved into what is today Oklahoma. The foragers collected seeds, nuts, roots, and berries. They hunted smaller animals than their predecessors, including deer, antelope, rabbits, wild turkey, and even mice. Remnants of their society have been discovered as well. Bags made of animal skin, sandals, rugs, and baskets have all been identified.

As time progressed, the native tribes living in Oklahoma began farming. Evidence suggests that farmers were living in the area as far back as 2,000 years ago. These natives lived in small villages and assisted each other in tending their crops and fields. They also helped each other defend their homes from any outside threats.

Cultivation of the ground was done by hand, using sticks and small tools made of stone or perhaps bone. Crops included corn, beans, squash, sunflowers, and tobacco. These tribes also hunted, using bows and arrows, as well as axes.

A little more than 500 years ago, the Spiro mound builders were living in far eastern Oklahoma. The Spiro were ancestors of the Caddo tribe and a considerable amount is known about the tribe today. The men were talented craftsmen, creating items from shells, copper, and stone. Women produced garments, bags, and blankets made from various types of animal fur and feathers.

The tribe amused themselves by playing a game called chunkey. Chunkey was popular amongst tribes across North America. It involved rolling a disc-shaped stone across the ground while participants attempted to throw spears as close to the stone as possible. The earliest explorers who encountered these tribes claimed that the natives would play this game endlessly during their free time.

> *Words to watch for:*
>
> *nomadic   forager*
>
> *remnants   cultivation*

The tribe is known as the mound builders because of one type of historic artifact they left behind. The Spiro Mounds are large mounds made of cedar logs which were covered by a significant amount of dirt. The dirt was brought in by hand, using baskets full of loose earth. Twelve mounds have been discovered in all. The purposes of these mounds are debated, but it is believed that two of them served as religious temples, while nine others were constructed as homes. One seems to have been built as a burial mound. In 1933, this burial mound was excavated by archaeologists. Many priceless artifacts were likely taken and sold by looters, but much valuable knowledge was still gained from the excavation of this site.

Today, the Spiro mounds can still be visited. The mounds are located at the Spiro Mounds State Archaeological Park just outside of Spiro, Oklahoma.

Multiple Choice: *Select the choice that completes the statement or answers the question.*

1._____ Which of the following best summarizes the earliest native settlers in Oklahoma?
a. The earliest settlers were farmers who raised beans, squash, sunflowers, and tobacco.
b. The earliest settlers were nomadic wanderers who hunted big game like the wooly mammoth.
c. The earliest settlers were French fur trappers who trapped raccoons and beaver.
d. The earliest settlers were Spanish conquistadors who believed there was gold in the area.

2._____ Which of the following is not evidence, found by archaeologists, of the Clovis people?
a. spear points and tar-lined bags made for carrying water
b. journals and logs left by Clovis hunters
c. mammoth skulls with painted markings
d. sites where mammoth were tracked down and killed

3._____ Which of the following best identifies crops raised by the farmers of 2,000 years ago?
a. corn, beans, squash, sunflowers, and tobacco
b. wheat, barley, rye, and potatoes
c. broccoli, okra, corn, tomatoes, and beets
d. milo, canola, peanuts, and sunflowers

4._____ Which of the following best summarizes the game known as chunkey?
a. It involved small sticks with baskets attached. The object of the game was to use the sticks to throw a ball into hoops at either end of the playing field.
b. It involved kicking a ball as far as they could and then racing to see who could reach it first.
c. It involved hitting a ball with a stick and running bases, very similar to baseball.
d. It involved rolling a disc-shaped stone, with participants throwing spears as close to the stone as possible.

5._____ Which of the following best describes the Spiro Mounds?
a. The Spiro Mounds were made of cedar logs covered with dirt. They were used for religious temples and burial mounds.
b. The Spiro Mounds were constructed of bricks and mortar. They were used as housing by ancestors of the Caddo.
c. The Spiro Mounds were supposedly made of solid gold. Although many archaeologists have searched for them, the mounds have never been found.
d. The Spiro Mounds were made entirely of ivory. They were used strictly as burial chambers for wealthy tribe members.

Vocabulary: *Match each word with its correct definition. Consider how the word is used in the lesson. This might help you define each term. Use a dictionary to help if necessary.*

a. nomad   d. remnants
b. archaeologist   e. cultivation
c. forage

6._____ small parts or fragments that are leftover

7._____ one who studies the artifacts and other remains of ancient cultures

8._____ a wanderer who has no established home and moves in search of food

9._____ the preparation of ground to promote the growth of crops

10._____ searching for food

Guided Reading: *Fill in the blanks below to create complete sentences.*

1. The earliest natives to live in Oklahoma were nomadic _____.

2. _____ have found considerable evidence of the Clovis peoples presence, as well as that of other ancient native tribes.

3. Foragers hunted smaller animals than their predecessors, including deer, antelope, _____, wild turkey, and even mice.

4. As time progressed, the native tribes living in Oklahoma began _____.

5. The tribes of about 2,000 years ago also hunted, using bows and _____, as well as axes.

6. The Spiro women produced garments, bags, and _____ made from various types of animal fur and feathers.

7. The tribe amused themselves by playing a game called _____.

8. _____ Spiro Mounds have been discovered in all.

9. Many priceless artifacts had been taken from the Spiro Mounds and sold by _____.

10. Today, the mounds are located at the Spiro Mounds State Archaeological Park, which is just outside of _____.

Summarize: *Answer the following questions in the space provided. Attempt to respond in a complete sentence for each question. Be sure to use correct capitalization and punctuation!*

1. Who were the Spiro Mound builders the ancestors of?

2. What did foragers collect?

3. When were the Spiro Mounds excavated?

4. Where was the first evidence of the Clovis tribes found?

5. Why do you suppose so much is known about the Spiro Mound builders today?

6. How was cultivation done 2,000 years ago?

Student Response: *Write a paragraph addressing the questions raised below. A thorough response should consist of three to five complete sentences.*

7. Why do you suppose it is so difficult for us to learn about ancient tribes that lived hundreds, or even thousands of years ago? Explain your answer as thoroughly as possible.

Francisco Coronado & Spanish Exploration

In the1500s, several Spaniards explored the southwest region of the United States. Who were these explorers? What were they searching for?

Francisco Coronado was a Spanish conquistador (conqueror) who arrived in New Spain (Mexico) in 1535. He was 25 years old and, like most other conquistadors, searching for gold and glory. Rumors had reached the Spaniards of fabulous cities off to the north. Legends claimed that these cities contained untold riches. The residents of these cities supposedly had so much gold that they ate their meals from golden plates and used golden utensils. The cities were known as Cíbola, or the seven cities of gold.

On February 23, 1540, Coronado set out with a large expedition of about 400 Spaniards, over 1,000 Mexican Indians, and a large number of family members and servants. The group took with them a large herd of cattle, sheep, and hogs, all of which were animals introduced to North America by the Spaniards.

They traveled throughout the southwest region of what is now the United States, exploring the regions that are Arizona and New Mexico today. Each step of the way, instead of cities of gold, they found simple Native American villages. Their hopes were frequently aroused by the distant sight of dwellings which appeared to shimmer as if made of gold. However, when they arrived, they found only adobe huts. The adobes were made of mud bricks, and an optical illusion caused the distant golden appearance.

At each village they visited, Coronado displayed little respect for the natives living there. He forced the villagers to carry his men's baggage and equipment, robbed them of their food, and even took tribal chiefs hostage.

Words to watch for:

conquistador   adobe

illusion   fabled

Eventually, Coronado was introduced to a native guide, The Turk. The Turk told Coronado of a different mythical city, the legendary golden city of Quivira. The Turk offered to guide Coronado and his expedition to this fabled city. Today, it is highly speculated that The Turk's true intention was simply to lead Coronado far away from his own people.

From there, The Turk led Coronado's expedition into the panhandle of Texas as well as Oklahoma, where Coronado took notes of what he observed. He and his men were awed by the vastness of the Great Plains. They saw enormous herds of buffalo, but few trees. In fact, there were so few trees that his men were reduced to using buffalo manure as fuel for their fires. He also observed a tribe of Apache who hunted the buffalo, ate the meat raw, and used the hides for tents and clothing.

Coronado and his men traveled into Kansas and crossed the Arkansas River. Eventually, they arrived at a Native American village (most likely ancestors of the Wichita). It was not a city of gold as Coronado had hoped for. Instead, he had found straw-thatched huts and fields of corn, beans, and squash. He and his party stayed with the villagers for twenty-five days, making observations and taking notes. Disappointed, Coronado had The Turk executed for deceiving him before returning to Mexico.

Friar Juan Padilla had traveled with Coronado during this first journey. After returning to Mexico, Friar Padilla hoped to Christianize the tribe they had visited. He, two of his followers, and a conquistador named Andres de Campo, set out to find the village once more. The villagers welcomed them warmly, and Friar Padilla had much success in his missionary work. Therefore, he and de Campo sought out another village. They found the Kaw tribe less receptive and Friar Padilla was killed. De Campo and Friar Padilla's followers returned to Mexico, traveling through large portions of Kansas, central Oklahoma, and Texas. Just as Coronado had done, they took extensive notes of all that they saw. The three men finally returned to Mexico five years after their journey had begun.

Juan de Oñate was another Spanish conquistador who was sure he could succeed where Coronado had failed. In 1601, he undertook his own expedition of the Great Plains in search of the fabled cities of gold. He explored the Canadian River region and saw vast prairies where "the grass was high enough to conceal a horse". Similar to Coronado's expedition, he found no cities of gold, only simple native villages.

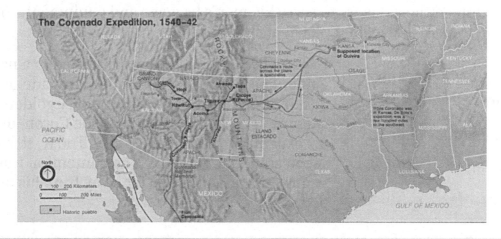

Multiple Choice: *Select the choice that completes the statement or answers the question.*

1._____ Which of the following statements about Francisco Coronado is *not* accurate?
a. Coronado had traveled to New Spain (Mexico) in search of gold and glory.
b. Coronado hoped to Christianize the natives while exploring North America.
c. Coronado was a 25-year-old conquistador when his journey began.
d. Coronado was searching for the Seven Cities of Cíbola.

2._____ Which of the following best summarizes how Coronado treated the Native Americans
        he encountered?
a. He had little respect for the natives, forcing them to carry his equipment while robbing them of their food.
b. Coronado was very friendly towards the natives and traded many items with them.
c. Coronado attempted to be friendly but was chased away by the Native Americans who attacked him.
d. Coronado did not encounter any Native Americans during his expedition.

3._____ Which of the following best describes the likely intentions of The Turk as he guided Coronado
        and his expedition?
a. The Turk hoped to lead them to the mythical city of Quívíra.
b. The Turk hoped to lead them into an ambush.
c. The Turk hoped that Coronado might take him back to Spain.
d. The Turk hoped to guide the Spaniards away from his own people.

4._____ Which of the following best summarizes the purpose of Juan Padilla's expedition?
a. Padilla was searching for the Seven Cities of Cíbola.
b. Padilla was searching for the Fountain of Youth.
c. Padilla was attempting to Christianize the Wichita Indians.
d. Padilla was attempting to locate the source of the Red River.

5._____ Which of the following statements about Juan de Oñate is *not* true?
a. Oñate was searching for the fabled cities of gold.
b. Oñate explored the Canadian River and saw massive grass prairies.
c. Oñate eventually climbed the Rocky Mountains.
d. Oñate found no cities of gold, only simple native villages.

Vocabulary: *Match each word with its correct definition. Consider how the word is used in the lesson. This might help you define each term. Use a dictionary to help if necessary.*

a. conquistador
b. adobe
c. illusion
d. Quívíra
e. fabled

6._____ a legendary mythical city of gold

7._____ a Spanish explorer who arrived in North America during the 1500s

8._____ a false or misleading impression of reality

9._____ a building made of sun-dried bricks

10._____ having no real existence; fictitious

Guided Reading: *Fill in the blanks below to create complete sentences.*

1. On February 23, 1540, Coronado set out with a large expedition of about 400 _____.

2. Coronado traveled throughout the American southwest, exploring the regions that are now Arizona and _____.

3. The Turk led Coronado's expedition into the panhandle of Texas as well as Oklahoma, where Coronado and his men were awed by the vastness of the _____.

4. Villagers welcomed Friar Padilla warmly, and he had much success in his _____ work.

5. Andres De Campo and Friar Padilla's followers returned to Mexico and took extensive _____ of all that they saw along the way.

Correct the Statement: *Each of the following sentences is false. Circle the incorrect word and write the word or phrase that makes the statement correct in the answer blank provided.*

6. Francisco Coronado was a conquistador from France. _____.

7. Coronado and his men were searching for the seven lost cities of silver. _____.

8. The Turk led Coronado's expedition into the panhandle of Texas and Nebraska. _____.

9. The Native Americans that Coronado found in Kansas were most likely ancestors of the Cherokee. _____.

10. Andres de Campo was a friar who hoped to Christianize the Wichita Indians. _____.

Summarize: *Answer the following questions in the space provided. Attempt to respond in a complete sentence for each question. Be sure to use correct capitalization and punctuation!*

1. Who guided Coronado when he was searching for Quivira?

2. What did Coronado find that resembled gold when spotted from a distance?

3. When did Coronado depart on his expedition?

4. Which present-day states did Coronado visit?

5. Why was The Turk executed?

6. How did Friar Padilla's expedition end?

Student Response: *Write a paragraph addressing the questions raised below. A thorough response should consist of three to five complete sentences.*

7. Why do you suppose the conquistadors were so willing to believe stories about cities made of gold? Explain your answer as thoroughly as possible.

French Exploration

The French once owned the large piece of land known as the Louisiana Territory. How did the French gain possession of this territory? What did they do with it?

Robert de LaSalle was a French explorer who arrived in North America in 1666. He established a series of forts along the Mississippi River. While exploring the Mississippi, he gave the name "Louisiana" to the territory lying west of the river and claimed it in the name of France. During his travels, he also established the outpost that would eventually become Little Rock, Arkansas. Despite never exploring the actual Louisiana Territory, his actions were significant because it gave France a claim to this vast expanse of land.

Robert de LaSalle

In 1718, Bernard LaHarpe left France with forty men. They arrived in North America with the intention of exploring the Louisiana Territory. LaHarpe and his men followed the Red River to where the present-day town of Idabel, Oklahoma is. They then turned north and headed through the Ouachita Mountains where they made contact with a band of Osage. After twenty-three days of travel, LaHarpe and his party came across a large Wichita settlement (just south of present-day Tulsa). They estimated that this village had between 6,000 and 7,000 people. They were greeted warmly by the village and spent several days amongst the Wichita.

> *Words to watch for:*
>
> *intention   extensive*
>
> *fertile   enterprise*

While traveling, LaHarpe took extensive notes of what he observed. According to his notes, the Wichita were excellent farmers and had tame horses. He also noted that the area was plentiful in wildlife. The forests were full of animals, and the streams and rivers were teeming with fish. The land itself was fertile and rich in minerals.

LaHarpe treated his hosts well, giving the local chiefs gifts of guns, knives, hatchets, and paint. As a result, the French were able to establish good trading relationships with the Native Americans of the region. In no time at all, French fur trappers and traders had moved into the region, hunting for buffalo hide, deer and beaver skins, and many other types of fur. By the 1760s, French fur traders such as Pierre Laclede and Auguste Chouteau had settled in the region and made the fur trade a valuable enterprise.

The work of these French explorers, trappers, and traders was significant, for they made the first extensive explorations of the area that would someday become Oklahoma. Their maps and notes proved to be valuable assets for the American explorers who would arrive in the early 1800s. Evidence of the French presence in Oklahoma can still be found in some town names. Sallisaw, Poteau, Chouteau, and Kiamichi are all town names with French origins.

Multiple Choice: *Select the choice that completes the statement or answers the question.*

1._____ Which of the following is not significant about Robert de LaSalle?
a. He established several forts along the Mississippi River.
b. He gave the name Louisiana to the area west of the Mississippi River.
c. He explored the Louisiana Territory and made detailed maps of the area.
d. He claimed Louisiana Territory for France.

2._____ Which of the following best summarizes Bernard LaHarpe's journey?
a. He followed the Red River, traveled through the Ouachita Mountains, and eventually found a large settlement of Wichita Indians.
b. He followed the Arkansas River, traveled through the Winding Stair Mountains, and eventually found a large settlement of Osage Indians.
c. He followed the Mississippi River and established several trading posts, one of which eventually became Little Rock, Arkansas.
d. He followed the Colorado River, traveled through the Rocky Mountains, and eventually reached the Pacific Ocean.

3._____ Which of the following accurately summarizes the notes LaHarpe made about his journey?
a. He noted that the Wichita were unfriendly, the area was virtually devoid of wildlife, and that the land was a barren desert.
b. He noted that there was little water, very few trees, and it was not fit for human habitation.
c. He noted that the local natives were very hostile, most of the wildlife was predatory in nature, and overall the territory was a very dangerous place.
d. He noted that the Wichita were excellent farmers, the area was plentiful in wildlife, and the land was fertile and rich in minerals.

4._____ Which of the following best describes the relationship between the French and Native Americans?
a. The French were rude to the Native Americans and had a difficult time getting along with them.
b. The French treated the Native Americans well and were able to establish good trade relations with them.
c. The French attacked the Native Americans immediately and attempted to chase them out of the area.
d. The French did not encounter any Native Americans during the earliest explorations of the Louisiana Territory.

5._____ Why are Pierre Laclede and Auguste Chouteau significant?
a. They were the first men to find the source of the Red River.
b. They established several forts on the Mississippi River, including New Orleans.
c. They were fur traders who settled in the region and made fur trading a valuable enterprise.
d. They were missionaries who worked in and amongst the Wichita for many years.

Guided Reading: *Fill in the blanks below to create complete sentences.*

1. Robert de LaSalle was a _____ explorer who had arrived in North America in 1666.

2. During LaSalle's travels, he also established the outpost that would eventually become _____, Arkansas.

3. LaHarpe and his men followed the Red River to where the present-day town of _____, Oklahoma is.

4. LaSalle and his party came across a large Wichita settlement which they estimated had between 6,000 and _____ people.

5. LaHarpe noted that the forests were full of animals, and the streams and rivers were teeming with _____.

6. LaHarpe treated his hosts well, giving the local chiefs _____ of guns, knives, hatchets, and paint.

7. In no time at all, French fur _____ and traders had moved into the region, hunting for buffalo hide, deer skins, beaver skins, and many other types of fur.

8. The work of these French explorers, trappers, and traders was significant, for they made the first extensive _____ of the area.

9. Evidence of the French presence in Oklahoma can still be found in some _____ names.

10. Sallisaw, _____, Chouteau, and Kiamichi are all town names with French origins.

Vocabulary: *Match each word with its correct definition. Consider how the word is used in the lesson. This might help you define each term. Use a dictionary to help if necessary.*

a. intention   d. enterprise
b. extensive   e. asset
c. fertile

11._____ far-reaching; comprehensive; thorough

12._____ the purpose or reason a certain action was done; goal

13._____ a useful or desirable thing

14._____ capable of producing vegetation

15._____ a commercial business

Name_____

Summarize: *Answer the following questions in the space provided. Attempt to respond in a complete sentence for each question. Be sure to use correct capitalization and punctuation.*

1. Who named the territory "Louisiana"?

2. What gifts did LaHarpe give to the local chiefs?

3. When did Robert de LaSalle arrive in North America?

4. Where did LaHarpe find the large settlement of Wichita?

5. Why were the French able to establish good trading relations with the Native Americans?

6. How were the efforts of the French explorers able to help the American explorers who arrived in the early 1800s?

Student Response: *Write a paragraph addressing the questions raised below. A thorough response should consist of three to five complete sentences.*

7. History shows us that the native tribes reacted to Spanish and French explorers very differently. Why might this have been the case? Explain your answer as thoroughly as possible.

The French had a major impact on the early exploration and settlement of Oklahoma. Bernard LaHarpe and many others explored the region, took many notes, and established settlements which are still part of the state today. Use a map of Oklahoma or internet sources to help you locate and label the following items which are mentioned in "French Exploration":

Mountains should be labeled with a ^^^^^^ symbol. Cities should be labeled with a •

Red River	Ouachita Mountains	Idabel	Tulsa
Sallisaw	Poteau	Chouteau	Kiamichi

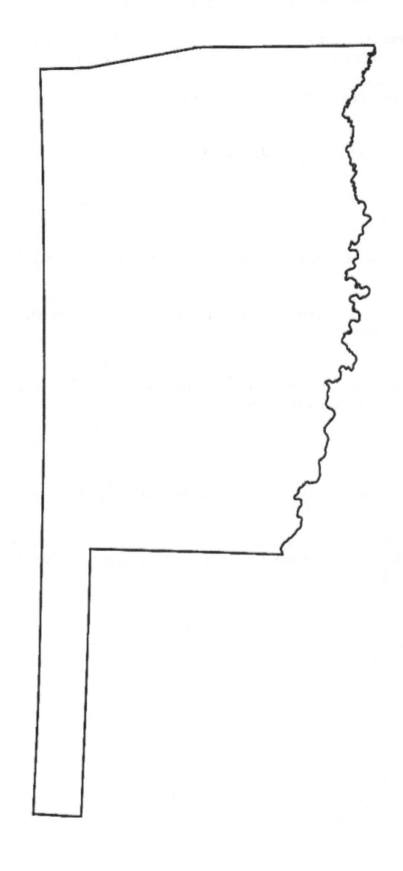

American Exploration

Many American explorers traveled through present-day Oklahoma. Who were these explorers? What was the purpose of their missions?

In 1803, the United States purchased the Louisiana Territory from France for $15 million. Shortly after this purchase, President Thomas Jefferson sent Meriwether Lewis & William Clark to explore the northern region of the territory. Other teams were assembled to explore the southern portion of Louisiana.

Zebulon Pike

One such expedition was led by Zebulon Pike. Pike was given instructions to find the source of the Arkansas River and Red River. While traveling, he was to make detailed maps of the region, determine the value of natural resources, and attempt to establish friendly relationships with Native Americans. This journey began on July 15th, 1806.

> *Words to watch for:*
>
> summit   comprehensive
>
> tributary   topography

In November, the team spotted the summit of an enormous mountain. Pike took a small number of men in an effort to climb this mountain. However, they underestimated its distance and were forced to turn back before reaching it. This mountain, Pike's Peak (in Colorado), bears his name today.

At one point during their journey, Pike and his men became lost, drifting into Spanish-held territory. They were captured and detained for a period of time before being released.

James Wilkinson was a part of the Pike Expedition. He and five others were given the task of exploring the Arkansas River while Pike and his men explored the Red. Their exploration of the Arkansas River began in the fall of 1806 and continued on through the winter months. They started in boats, but were reduced to walking because of dry river beds. Even where water existed, the boats became useless because the rivers were frozen over. They were forced to cut through the ice using axes.

As their journey wore on, they suffered from frostbite and lack of food. They were out of ammunition, which meant they could not hunt. The group managed to survive by trading with friendly Osage Indians who were camped out on the river's edge.

In 1811, George Sibley, an agent of the U.S. government, was sent to negotiate with the Osage. During his negotiations, he and a group of about twenty others explored the territory. While searching, he discovered a region that was "glistening like a field of snow in the summer sun." He had discovered the Great Salt Plains. He wrote in his notes that there was an "inexhaustible supply of ready-made salt." With additional exploration, Sibley discovered even more salt, the Big Salt Plain, near present-day Freedom, Oklahoma.

Stephen Long

In 1820, Stephen H. Long and John Bell led another expedition through what is today Oklahoma. The Long-Bell Expedition had a similar goal to the Pike Expedition. Explore the Red River and Arkansas River, and map out the area.

John Bell and his twelve men explored the Arkansas River. They traveled through portions of Oklahoma during the hot summer months. They faced temperatures of more than one hundred degrees and found little water. Hunting was difficult because no animals could be found. When the team finally returned to Fort Smith, they were hungry and exhausted.

Stephen Long took the other half of the expedition to explore the Red River. They became lost and ended up on the Canadian River instead (a tributary to the Arkansas). However, they took comprehensive notes of the region's topography. Long observed that there was little timber for home building, virtually no surface water, and vast herds of bison. He claimed that the region was not fit for settlement by anyone dependent upon agriculture and referred to the area as "a great desert." It was from this description that the phrase "The Great American Desert" became widely used.

One final exploration of the state was done by Thomas Nuttall. Nuttall was an English botanist who studied the wide variety of plant and animal life he observed. With the help of native guides, he explored many different regions, from the Great Salt Plains, to the Osage prairies, and the Cimarron River.

Multiple Choice: *Select the choice that completes the statement or answers the question.*

1._____ Which of the following best summarizes the purpose of Zebulon Pike's
expedition?
a. He was to find Pike's Peak and climb it.
b. He was to find the source of the Arkansas and Red Rivers, make detailed
maps, and determine the value of natural resources.
c. He was to find the source of the Mississippi River and establish friendly
relationships with Native American tribes.
d. He was to find deposits of salt and silver, as well search for the mythical
cities of gold that Coronado had searched for.

2._____ Which of the following best summarizes the expedition led by
Lt. James Wilkinson?
a. They explored the Arkansas River through the winter months, facing extreme
cold and ice.
b. They explored the Red River through the summer months, facing extreme heat
with little water.
c. They explored the Canadian River through the spring and thought the region
was wonderful.
d. They explored the Arkansas River through the fall months and became hopelessly lost.

3._____ Which of the following significant discoveries did George Sibley make?
a. He discovered the Sibley Falls, which is the tallest waterfall in North America.
b. He discovered Sibley Peak, which is the tallest mountain west of the Mississippi River.
c. He discovered the Great Plains and gave it the nickname "the Great American Desert".
d. He discovered the Great Salt Plains, "an inexhaustible supply of ready-made salt."

4._____ Which of the following best summarizes what Stephen Long described during
his journey through the Louisiana Territory?
a. He described it as one of the most beautiful places he had ever seen, with
many trees and abundant wildlife.
b. He described it as a great desert, with little timber or surface water, and not
fit for settlement or agriculture.
c. He described it as a frozen tundra, with very little water and no plant life.
d. He described it as a perfect spot for farming, with thousands of acres of flat
ground and fertile fields.

5._____ Which of the following best describes Thomas Nuttall's contribution to
exploring the Louisiana Territory?
a. He was the first to see the Gloss Mountains and gave them their name.
b. He discovered the source of the Arkansas River and followed it back to the Mississippi.
c. He located the Great Salt Plains and took extensive notes about the region.
d. He studied the wide variety of plant and animal life found in the Louisiana Territory.

Vocabulary: *Match each word with its correct definition. Consider how the word is used in the lesson. This might help you define each term. Use a dictionary to help if necessary.*

a. summit   d. topography
b. comprehensive   e. botanist
c. tributary

1._____ a stream that flows into a larger river

2._____ a scientist who studies plant life

3._____ a large scope; covering or involving much; all-inclusive

4._____ the land forms or surface features of a region

5._____ the highest point of a hill or mountain

Guided Reading: *Fill in the blanks below to create complete sentences.*

6. In 1803, the United States purchased the Louisiana Territory from France for _____.

7. Pike was given instructions to find the _____ of the Arkansas River and Red River.

8. Pike took a small number of men, hoping to climb _____, which is named after him today.

9. At one point during their journey, Pike and his men became lost, drifting into _____-held territory.

10. James Wilkinson and his men started in _____, but were reduced to walking because of dry river beds.

Correct the Statement: *Each of the following sentences is false. Circle the incorrect word and write the word or phrase that makes the statement correct in the answer blank provided.*

11. George Sibley was an agent of the U.S. Government who was sent to negotiate with the Apache. _____.

12. Stephen H. Long and John Bell were to explore the Red River and Canadian River and map out the area. _____.

13. John Bell and his twelve men traveled through portions of Oklahoma during the hot winter months. _____.

14. Stephen Long and his expedition were to explore the Red River, but they became lost and ended up on the Colorado River instead. _____.

15. Thomas Nuttall was a biologist who studied the wide variety of plant and animal life he observed. _____.

Summarize: *Answer the following questions in the space provided. Attempt to respond in a complete sentence for each question. Be sure to use correct capitalization and punctuation!*

1. Who was sent to explore the northern region of the Louisiana Territory?

2. What phrase came to be widely used to describe the region that Stephen Long explored?

3. When did Zebulon Pike's journey begin?

4. Where is the Big Salt Plain?

5. Why did Stephen Long not feel that the area was fit for settlement?

6. How did James Wilkinson's expedition manage to survive?

Student Response: *Write a paragraph addressing the questions raised below. A thorough response should consist of three to five complete sentences.*

7. Stephen Long referred to part of the Louisiana Territory as "a great desert" and stated that it was not fit for settlement. How was his opinion of the region shaped? Cite specific textual evidence to help support your answer.

Zebulon Pike, James Wilkinson, Stephen Long, and others were given instructions to explore many of the waterways through Oklahoma. Use a map of Oklahoma, or internet sources, to help you locate and label the following items which are mentioned in "American Exploration":

Rivers should be drawn in and labeled. Cities should be labeled with a •

Arkansas River   Red River   Great Salt Plains   Freedom
Canadian River   Cimarron River   Big Salt Plain   Osage Prairie

Name_____

There are many rivers that run through Oklahoma. Most of these were explored during the early era of American exploration. Utilize a map and internet resources to help you locate and label the following waterways.

Rivers should be drawn in using blue.

Red River	Arkansas River	Cimarron River	Canadian River
North Canadian River	Deep Fork River	North Fork Red River	Illinois River

Early History: Post Assessment

Vocabulary: *Match each word with its correct definition.*

a. conquistador
b. adobe
c. tributary
d. Quivira

e. nomad
f. topography
g. cultivate
h. archaeologist

1._____ a stream that flows into a large river

2._____ the land forms or surface features of a region

3._____ one who studies artifacts and other remains of ancient cultures

4._____ a wanderer who has no established home and moves in search of food

5._____ the preparation of ground to promote the growth of crops

6._____ a legendary mythical city of gold

7._____ a Spanish explorer who arrived in North America in the 1500s

8._____ a building made of sun-dried bricks

Multiple Choice: *Select the choice that completes the statement or answers the question.*

9._____ Which of the following best summarizes the earliest native settlers in Oklahoma?
a. The earliest settlers were farmers who raised beans, squash, sunflowers, and tobacco.
b. The earliest settlers were nomadic wanderers who hunted big game like the wooly mammoth.
c. The earliest settlers were French fur trappers who trapped raccoons and beaver.
d. The earliest settlers were Spanish conquistadors who believed there was gold in the area.

10._____ Which of the following is not evidence, found by archaeologists, of the Clovis people?
a. spear points and tar-lined bags made for carrying water
b. journals and logs left by Clovis hunters
c. mammoth skulls with painted markings
d. sites where mammoth were tracked down and killed

11._____ Which of the following best explains why the Clovis tribes are known by this name?
a. It was well-known that this tribe had affection for the beautiful clovis flower.
b. The first known settlements of these tribes were discovered by Richard Clovis.
c. The first known settlements of these tribes were discovered near Clovis, New Mexico.
d. It was well-known that this tribe depended heavily on the now extinct clovis buffalo.

12._____ Which of the following best summarizes the game known as chunkey?
a. It involved small sticks with baskets attached. The object of the game was to use the sticks to throw a ball into hoops at either end of the playing field.
b. It involved kicking a ball as far as they could and then racing to see who could reach it first.
c. It involved hitting a ball with a stick and running bases, very similar to baseball.
d. It involved rolling a disc-shaped stone, with participants throwing spears as close to the stone as possible.

13._____ Which of the following best describes the Spiro Mounds?
a. The Spiro Mounds were made of cedar logs covered with dirt. They were used for religious temples and burial mounds.
b. The Spiro Mounds were constructed of bricks and mortar. They were used as housing by ancestors of the Caddo.
c. The Spiro Mounds were supposedly made of solid gold. Although many archaeologists have searched for them, the mounds have never been found.
d. The Spiro Mounds were made entirely of ivory. They were used strictly as burial chambers for wealthy tribe members.

14._____ The Spiro Mound builders were ancestors of which of the following tribes?
a. Caddo
b. Apache
c. Sioux
d. Iroquois

15._____ Which of the following best summarizes how Coronado treated the Native Americans he encountered?
a. He had little respect for the natives, forcing them to carry his equipment while robbing them of their food.
b. Coronado was very friendly towards the natives and traded many items with them.
c. Coronado attempted to be friendly, but was chased away by the Native Americans who attacked him.
d. Coronado did not encounter any Native Americans during his expedition.

16._____ Which of the following correctly identifies what Coronado saw, which resembled gold from a distance?
a. He saw the heat rising off the desert sand, which caused everything to shimmer.
b. He saw deposits of quartz crystals which reflected off the sun.
c. He saw deposits of iron pyrite, also known as fool's gold.
d. He saw the walls of adobe huts, which shimmered in the sunlight.

17._____ Which of the following correctly identifies Coronado's guide as he traveled throughout the Southwest?
a. The Turk
b. Pocahontas
c. Sacajawea
d. Squanto

18._____ Which of the following best describes the likely intentions of The Turk as he guided Coronado and his expedition?
a. The Turk hoped to lead them to the mythical city of Quívíra.
b. The Turk hoped to lead them into an ambush.
c. The Turk hoped that Coronado might take him back to Spain.
d. The Turk hoped to guide the Spaniards away from his own people.

19._____ Which of the following best summarizes the purpose of Juan Padilla's expedition?
a. Padilla was searching for the Seven Cities of Cíbola.
b. Padilla was searching for the Fountain of Youth.
c. Padilla was attempting to Christianize the Wichita Indians.
d. Padilla was attempting to locate the source of the Red River.

20._____ How did the expedition of Friar Juan Padilla come to an end?
a. He decided to remain with the Wichita Indians.
b. He was executed by the Kaw Indians.
c. He traveled further north and was never heard from again.
d. He returned to Mexico and was celebrated as a hero.

21._____ Which of the following is not significant about Robert de LaSalle?
a. He established several forts along the Mississippi River.
b. He gave the name Louisiana to the area west of the Mississippi River.
c. He explored the Louisiana Territory and made detailed maps of the area.
d. He claimed Louisiana Territory for France.

22._____ Which of the following best summarizes Bernard LaHarpe's journey?
a. He followed the Red River, traveled through the Ouachita Mountains, and eventually found a large settlement of Wichita Indians.
b. He followed the Arkansas River, traveled through the Winding Stair Mountains, and eventually found a large settlement of Osage Indians.
c. He followed the Mississippi River and established several trading posts, one of which eventually became Little Rock, Arkansas.
d. He followed the Colorado River, traveled through the Rocky Mountains, and eventually reached the Pacific Ocean.

23._____ Which of the following accurately summarizes the notes LaHarpe made about his journey?
a. He noted that the Wichita were unfriendly, the area was virtually devoid of wildlife, and that the land was a barren desert.
b. He noted that there was little water, very few trees, and it was not fit for human habitation.
c. He noted that the local natives were very hostile, most of the wildlife was predatory in nature, and overall the territory was a very dangerous place.
d. He noted that the Wichita were excellent farmers, the area was plentiful in wildlife, and the that land was fertile and rich with minerals.

24._____ Which of the following was not amongst the items Bernard LaHarpe gave to local chiefs?
a. guns
b. knives
c. gold
d. paint

25._____ Which of the following best describes the relationship between the French and Native Americans?
a. The French were rude to the Native Americans and had a difficult time with them.
b. The French treated the Native Americans well and established good trade relations.
c. The French attacked the Native Americans immediately, trying to chase them from the area.
d. The French did not encounter any Native Americans during their earliest explorations.

26._____ Why are Pierre Laclede and Auguste Chouteau significant?
a.   They were the first men to find the source of the Red River.
b.   They established several forts on the Mississippi River, including New Orleans.
c.   They were fur traders who settled in the region and made fur trading a valuable enterprise.
d.   They were missionaries who worked in and amongst the Wichita for many years.

27._____ Which of the following best summarizes the purpose of Zebulon Pike's expedition?
a.   He was to find Pike's Peak and climb it.
b.   He was to find the source of the Arkansas and Red Rivers, make detailed maps,
     and determine the value of natural resources.
c.   He was to find the source of the Mississippi River and establish friendly
     relationships with Native American tribes.
d.   He was to find deposits of salt and silver, as well search for the mythical cities of
     gold that Coronado had searched for.

28._____ Which of the following best summarizes the expedition led by Lt. James Wilkinson?
a.   They explored the Arkansas River through the winter months, facing extreme cold and ice.
b.   They explored the Red River through the summer months, facing extreme heat with little water.
c.   They explored the Canadian River through the spring and thought the region was wonderful.
d.   They explored the Arkansas River through the fall months and became hopelessly lost.

29._____ Which of the following significant discoveries did George Sibley make?
a.   He discovered the Sibley Falls, which is the tallest waterfall in North America.
b.   He discovered Sibley Peak, which is the tallest mountain west of the Mississippi River.
c.   He discovered the Great Plains and gave it the nickname "the Great American Desert".
d.   He discovered the Great Salt Plains, "an inexhaustible supply of ready-made salt."

30._____ Which of the following best summarizes what Stephen Long described during
           his journey through the Louisiana Territory?
a.   He described it as one of the most beautiful places he had ever seen, with many
     trees and abundant wildlife.
b.   He described it as a great desert, with little timber or surface water, and not fit for
     settlement or agriculture.
c.   He described it as a frozen tundra, with very little water and no plant life.
d.   He described it as a perfect spot for farming, with thousands of acres of flat
     ground and fertile fields.

31._____Which of the following correctly identifies the nickname given to present-day
           Oklahoma as a result of Stephen Long's exploration?
a.   The Vast Wasteland   c.   The Dust Bowl
b.   The Great American Desert   d.   The Great American Prairie

32._____ Which of the following best describes Thomas Nuttall's contribution to
           exploring the Louisiana Territory?
a.   He was the first to see the Gloss Mountains and gave them their name.
b.   He discovered the source of the Arkansas River and followed it back to the Mississippi.
c.   He located the Great Salt Plains and took extensive notes about the region.
d.   He studied the wide variety of plant and animal life found in the Louisiana Territory.

Completion: *Fill in the blanks below to create complete sentences.*

| Archaeologists | explorations | $15 million | New Mexico |
| Pike's Peak | own | French | Great Plains |

33. _____ have found considerable evidence of the Clovis peoples presence, as well as that of other ancient native tribes.

34. Francisco Coronado traveled throughout the American southwest, exploring the regions that are now Arizona and _____.

35. The Turk led Coronado's expedition into the panhandle of Texas as well as Oklahoma, where Coronado and his men were awed by the vastness of the _____.

36. Robert de LaSalle was a _____ explorer who had arrived in North America in 1666.

37. The work of these French explorers, trappers, and traders was significant, for they made the first extensive _____ of the area.

38. Evidence of the French presence in Oklahoma can still be found in some _____ names.

39. In 1803, the United States purchased the Louisiana Territory from France for

_____.

40. Zebulon Pike took a small number of men, hoping to climb _____, which is named after him today.

The Cherokee

The Cherokee were the largest of the Five Civilized Tribes. What were the Cherokee like prior to the arrival of Europeans? Does the Cherokee Nation still exist today?

The Cherokee have a long and storied history. Little is known about Cherokee life prior to the arrival of European settlers because Native Americans kept no written records. All histories of the various tribes were passed down orally. It is believed that the Cherokee more than likely migrated from the Great Lakes region at some time in their distant past. This is believed because the Cherokee language closely resembles the Iroquois languages that were prominent in that region.

Some historians believe that the Cherokee did not arrive in the Appalachia region until sometime during the 1200s. From there, the Cherokee eventually settled in what would become North Carolina, South Carolina, Tennessee, Georgia, and Alabama. However, there is much disagreement over when the migration to the Appalachian region occurred.

Words to watch for:

migration   decimated

epidemic   inevitable

Cherokee societal structure was divided into two groups, the "white" and the "red". The white organization was a group of elders who represented the seven different clans. These elders were responsible for religious activities such as healing and purification. The red organization was made up of younger men and they were responsible for warfare.

The Cherokee first came into contact with Europeans when Hernando de Soto visited in 1540. From that time on, contact with white settlers became more and more common. The Spaniards built several forts in the region throughout the late 1500s, but never established a long-term presence in the region. The Cherokee's first contact with English settlers came in 1654. The Cherokee fought with and drove off settlers who had attempted to settle land in Virginia.

Similar to all native tribes, as the Cherokee came in contact with Europeans, their numbers were decimated by disease. The Europeans brought foreign diseases with them, for which the Cherokee had no immunity. For example, in 1738 and 1739, an epidemic of smallpox wiped out nearly half of the Cherokee population.

The earliest white settlers to encounter the Cherokee recorded their observations about the tribe. They stated that the Cherokee had heavily-painted and tattooed skin, and their heads were shaved, except for a patch at the back of the skull. Their ears were stretched to enormous size and were adorned with silver pendants and rings. Similar pendants and rings were also worn on the nose.

Those who could afford it wore a collar of wampum (beads cut out of clam shells). Silver breastplates and silver bracelets were also worn. Clothing consisted of bits of cloth and large garments that hung over the entire body. They wore soft leather moccasins on their feet, usually made from deerskin.

As the tribe continued to have more and more contact with white settlers, they continued to adopt more white customs. The adoption of European customs is what led to the Cherokee and other tribes becoming known as the Civilized Tribes.

European clothing and names all became commonplace amongst the Cherokee (for example, the famous Cherokee Sequoyah was also known by the name George Guess). The Cherokee also adopted European farming methods and other advanced technologies.

The Cherokee were not one single tribe. Instead, it was a loose confederation with each group having autonomy over their own village. In 1735, there were approximately sixty-four such towns and villages of Cherokee. As time progressed, they adopted more formal structures of government. In the 1820s, the Cherokee even adopted a written constitution.

During the era of Indian Removal, the Cherokee became divided into two groups, the mixed-bloods and the full-bloods. This had little to do with ancestry or bloodlines. In fact, these groups were more closely related to modern political parties. The full-bloods were more traditional and hoped to hold on to the old ways and customs. They strongly opposed the removal process.

The mixed-bloods embraced more European customs than the full-bloods did. The mixed-bloods were not necessarily in favor of removal, but accepted it as being inevitable. They believed they should negotiate with the US government and get as much compensation for their lands as possible.

The rift between the mixed-bloods and the full-bloods continued after the tribe's arrival in Indian Territory. The feud continued even through the years of the Civil War. However, the Cherokee Nation eventually did begin to prosper once more.

Today, the Cherokee Nation has more than 300,000 members. It is the largest federally-recognized Native American tribe in the United States. Additionally, there are another 500,000 who claim Cherokee ancestry but are not official members of the tribe. The Cherokee Nation's headquarters are located in Tahlequah, Oklahoma.

Multiple Choice: *Select the choice that completes the statement or answers the question.*

1._____ Which of the following most accurately reflects why little is known about the Cherokee prior to the arrival of European settlers?
a.   The Cherokee are very secretive and do not tell outsiders about their tribal history.
b.   Most of the Cherokee records from that time period were lost in a great fire.
c.   The Cherokee, like other Native American tribes, did not keep written records.
d.   The Cherokee tribe did not exist until very recently.

2._____ Which of the following best identifies why it is believed that the Cherokee originally came from the Great Lakes region?
a.   There have been many artifacts found in Cherokee villages that were made from trees that are only found in the Great Lakes region.
b.   There are many stories amongst the Cherokee about a great migration that occurred in the 1200s.
c.   There is a religious belief that all Native American tribes originated from the Great Lakes region.
d.   The Cherokee language closely resembles Iroquois languages from the Great Lakes region.

3._____ In Cherokee society, which of the following best identifies the responsibilities of the "white" organization?
a.   This was a group of elders who were responsible for religious activities.
b.   This was a group of younger men responsible for warfare.
c.   This was a group of elders who were responsible for warfare.
d.   This was a group of younger men who were responsible for religious activities.

4._____ Which of the following best identifies why the Cherokee population was decimated by the arrival of European settlers?
a.   The European settlers were vicious and murdered the Cherokee by the thousands.
b.   Many of the Cherokee simply left, not wanting to deal with the new arrivals.
c.   European diseases, which the Cherokee had no immunity to, wiped out thousands.
d.   Many of the Cherokee abandoned their tribal lives and moved to the cities.

5._____ Which of the following properly identifies the two competing groups of Cherokee during the Indian Removal process?
a.   The white and the red
b.   The traditionalists and the progressives
c.   The full-bloods and the mixed-bloods
d.   The Bear Party and the Moose Party

Vocabulary: *Match each word with its correct definition. Consider how the word is used in the lesson. This might help you define each term. Use a dictionary to help if necessary.*

a.   migration
b.   decimate
c.   epidemic
d.   autonomy
e.   inevitable

6._____   self-governing; independent

7._____   the process of a large group of people moving from one place to another

8._____   unable to be avoided; sure to happen

9._____   to destroy a great number of

10._____   a disease that affects many people at the same time

Guided Reading: *Fill in the blanks below to create complete sentences.*

1. All histories of the various tribes were passed down _____.

2. Some historians believe that the Cherokee did not arrive in the
_____ region until sometime during the 1200s.

3. The Cherokee first came into contact with Europeans when _____
visited in 1540.

4. The earliest white settlers stated that the Cherokee had heavily-painted and
_____ skin.

5. The adoption of European customs is what led to the Cherokee and other tribes
becoming known as the _____ Tribes.

6. The Cherokee were a loose _____, with each group having
autonomy over their own village.

7. The full-bloods were more _____ and hoped to hold on to the
old ways and customs.

8. The mixed-bloods embraced more _____ customs than the full-
bloods did.

9. The feud between the mixed-bloods and full-bloods continued even through the years
of the _____.

10. Today, the Cherokee Nation has more than _____ members.

Summarize: *Answer the following questions in the space provided. Attempt to respond in a complete sentence for each question. Be sure to use correct capitalization and punctuation!*

1. Who was not necessarily in favor of removal, but accepted it as inevitable?

2. What was the "red" organization responsible for in Cherokee society?

3. When did the Cherokee adopt a written constitution?

4. Where is the headquarters of the Cherokee Nation?

5. Why did the mixed-bloods believe the Cherokee should negotiate with the US government?

6. How did the Cherokee dress when they were first observed by European settlers?

Student Response: *Write a paragraph addressing the questions raised below. A thorough response should consist of three to five complete sentences.*

7. Do you feel that the Cherokee were right in giving up their traditional ways to adopt more European customs? Would you have been a mixed-blood or a full-blood during the Indian Removal process?

The Cherokee lived in the southern portion of the United States. Use a map of the United States or internet resources to help you locate and label the following places which are mentioned in "The Cherokee".

Mountains should be labeled with the ^^^^^ symbol. Cities should be labeled with a •

Appalachian Mountains	North Carolina	South Carolina	Tennessee
Georgia	Alabama	Virginia	Tahlequah

Color each labeled state a different color.

The Choctaw

One of the Five Civilized Tribes was the Choctaw. Where did the Choctaw come from? Where are they today?

The Choctaw originally lived in the modern-day states of Louisiana, Mississippi, Alabama, and Florida. However, they weren't always known as the Choctaw. Choctaw ancestors were part of the Mississippian cultures which lived throughout the Mississippi River Valley region. Choctaw oral histories suggest that these ancestors lived in this region as far back as 4,000 to 8,000 years ago.

Archaeological evidence allows historians to speculate that the Choctaw did not actually emerge as a tribe until the 1600s. It was at that time when several different bands coalesced and began referring to themselves as Choctaw. The word "Choctaw" more than likely comes from a term in the Choctaw language, *Hacha hatak,* which means "river people".

Pushmataha

Hernando de Soto was the first European explorer to come in contact with Choctaw ancestors. The initial contact was not friendly. De Soto took Chief Tuskaloosa hostage and made many demands. In retaliation, the Choctaw attacked de Soto.

> **Words to watch for:**
>
> emerge   retaliation
>
> coalesced   matrilineal

In the earliest days of the United States, President George Washington initiated a plan to "civilize" and improve Native American society. Part of this plan included the hiring of government agents to live amongst the Choctaw and teach them how to live like European Americans. This Europeanization eventually led to the Choctaw being thought of as one of the Civilized Tribes. Scotch-Irish fur traders also lived in and amongst the Choctaw. These individuals collected detailed observations about Choctaw life.

For amusement, the Choctaw played a game known as stickball. The game was played with a small ball made of deer hair, stuffed tightly inside deerskin. The objective was to move the ball down the field of play and into a hoop, using sticks with small baskets attached. The game was extremely popular and most Native American tribes played a version of this sport. It could become increasingly violent. So much so, that some tribes referred to the game as "little war". The sport was eventually altered by Europeans and is still played today in the form of Lacrosse.

The Choctaw had a matrilineal society, just as many other native tribes did. This meant that the female was the head of the household, and all inheritance and family prestige was passed down through the female side of the family. This was in stark contrast to the European system, which was strictly patrilineal. Many Scotch-Irish traders married high-ranking Choctaw females, and as such, their children were automatically deemed prestigious members of Choctaw society. Many of these children went on to be leaders amongst the Choctaw and influenced relations with the United States in the early 1800s.

In 1811, the Choctaw leader Pushmataha was approached by the Shawnee leader Tecumseh. Tecumseh encouraged Pushmataha to fight against the United States. Pushmataha refused, stating that the Choctaw had always had a good relationship with the white men. Just nine years later, in 1820, Pushmataha was forced to sign the Treaty of Doak's Stand. According to the terms of this treaty, the Choctaw were required to cede nearly half of all their lands to the United States. In exchange, they were given land in Indian Territory. This was one of the early treaties that launched the Indian Removal process throughout the 1820s and 30s. Eventually, the Choctaw signed nine different treaties as they gave up more and more of their tribal lands. Despite this, many Choctaw managed to remain in Mississippi.

Today, the Choctaw are the third largest federally-recognized Native American tribe. There are actually two Choctaw nations, the Choctaw Nation of Oklahoma and the Mississippi Band of Choctaw Indians. Between these two, there are approximately 160,000 members of the Choctaw Nation.

Multiple Choice: *Select the choice that completes the statement or answers the question.*

1._____ Which of the following best traces the origins of Choctaw ancestors?
a.   Choctaw ancestors lived in the Great Lakes region before migrating south.
b.   Choctaw ancestors lived in the west, migrating east about 4,000 years ago.
c.   Choctaw ancestors lived in the Mississippi River Valley as far back as 8,000 years.
d.   Choctaw ancestors lived in South America, migrating north in search of cooler temperatures.

2._____ Which of the following best explains what the word "Choctaw" likely means?
a.   *Hacha hatak* is derived from the Choctaw language and means "river people".
b.   *Chac tah* is derived from the Muskogee language and means "lost wanderers".
c.   *Ch' oc-toh* is derived from an ancient Iroquois dialect and means "fellow traveler".
d.   *Choctaw* is the title given to them by English settlers because their native name was unpronounceable.

3._____ Which of the following best summarizes George Washington's approach to dealing with the
         Native American way of life?
a.   Washington hoped to move Native Americans west so that their way of life would not be disrupted.
b.   Washington declared war with the intention of eradicating natives from North America.
c.   Washington took them as slaves and sold thousands of Native Americans into slavery in Europe.
d.   Washington assigned government agents to live amongst the tribes and teach them how to live like
     European Americans.

4._____ Which of the following best describes a matrilineal society?
a.   A society in which the male is the head of the household, and all inheritance is passed through the
     male's family.
b.   A society in which the female is the head of the household, and all inheritance is passed through the
     female's family.
c.   A society in which each male is allowed to marry as many wives as he would like, as long as he is
     capable of providing for them.
d.   A society in which the female is allowed to marry as many husbands as she would like, as long as she
     is capable of taking care of them all.

5._____ Which of the following best summarizes the Treaty of Doak's Stand?
a.   The Choctaw agreed to cease all hostilities against the US government.
b.   The Choctaw agreed to pay the United States $3 million to continue living on their tribal lands.
c.   The Choctaw agreed to cede nearly half of their tribal lands to the United States.
d.   The Choctaw agreed to join the United States and enter the Union as the state of Mississippi.

Vocabulary: *Match each word with its correct definition. Consider how the word is used in the lesson.*
This might help you define each term. Use a dictionary to help if necessary.

a.   emerge   d.   matrilineal
b.   retaliation   e.   inheritance
c.   coalesce

6._____ property passed from one to another after someone's death

7._____ to take action for some injury or wrong; to avenge

8._____ to grow together; become one mass

9._____ to rise up or come forth

10._____ a societal structure based on the female's family line

Guided Reading: *Fill in the blanks below to create complete sentences.*

1. Choctaw ancestors were part of the _____ cultures.

2. Archaeological evidence allows historians to speculate that the Choctaw did not actually emerge as a tribe until the _____.

3. Hernando de Soto took Chief _____ hostage and made many demands. In retaliation, the Choctaw attacked de Soto.

4. _____ fur traders lived in and amongst the Choctaw.

5. The objective of stickball was to move the ball down the field of play and into a hoop, using sticks with small _____ attached.

6. Stickball was eventually altered by Europeans and is still played today in the form of _____.

7. The Choctaw matrilineal society was in stark contrast to the European system, which was a _____ society.

8. Scotch-Irish traders married high-ranking Choctaw _____, and their children were automatically deemed prestigious members of Choctaw society.

9. The Choctaw signed nine different treaties with the government, giving up more and more of their _____ lands.

10. Today, there are two Choctaw nations, the Choctaw Nation of _____ and the Mississippi Band of Choctaw Indians.

Summarize: *Answer the following questions in the space provided. Attempt to respond in a complete sentence for each question. Be sure to use correct capitalization and punctuation!*

1. Who refused to fight against the United States?

2. What was the name of the removal treaty the Choctaw were forced to sign in 1820?

3. When did the Shawnee chief Tecumseh approach Pushmataha about fighting the United States?

4. Where did the Choctaw originally live? (Which modern-day states?)

5. Why did some tribes refer to stickball as "little war"?

6. How did Pushmataha justify not fighting a war against the United States?

Student Response: *Write a paragraph addressing the questions raised below. A thorough response should consist of three to five complete sentences.*

7. Why do you suppose Hernando de Soto's first contact with the Native American tribes went so poorly? Try to consider the issue from both perspectives.

The Chickasaw

The Chickasaw were one of the Five Civilized Tribes. What were some of the Chickasaw practices and beliefs? How many Chickasaw are there today?

The Chickasaw are a Native American tribe that once lived in present-day Mississippi, Alabama, and Tennessee. It is unknown where the Chickasaw originated from, but their ancestors lived in the Mississippi River Valley for thousands of years. There are oral histories amongst the Chickasaw indicating that their prehistoric ancestors moved into the valley from the western portion of the continent.

Historians are also unsure when the Chickasaw emerged as tribe. Some suggest this happened as late as the 1600s (approximately the same time the Choctaw developed as a tribe). However, there is a Chickasaw legend that claims the Chickasaw rose up from a large earthwork mound called Nanih Waiya, which was constructed in about the year 300. The Choctaw have a similar story about this same mound.

Most beliefs amongst the Chickasaw were similar to those of other native tribes. Tales related to creation, and other events deemed important, were passed down orally in the form of stories. These stories would often feature various animals with each having a different significance based on the tribe and region in which they lived. For example, the legend known as "Ghost of the White Deer" explained why this animal was sacred to the Chickasaw. A trickster rabbit named Chokfi also featured in many children's stories. These tales would often have a moral or important lesson for the children.

Many of the native tribes, including the Chickasaw, were polygamous. This meant that each man was allowed to marry more than one wife. In some cases, the male was required to ask permission of the female before he could take another wife. In Chickasaw society, polygamy was not only allowed, but necessary. The tribe was so warlike and aggressive that their male population was in a perpetual state of depletion.

The Chickasaw's ancestors first encountered Europeans when Hernando de Soto arrived in 1540. The tribe was quite sophisticated at that time, having their own laws and governmental system. Unfortunately, de Soto and the Chickasaw had several disagreements which ended with the Chickasaw attacking the Spaniards in a nighttime raid.

Words to watch for:
polygamy   perpetual
assimilation compensated

As white settlers moved into the southeastern portion of what is today the United States (in the 1700s), the Chickasaw grew more accustomed to their presence. Eventually the tribe experienced the same process of assimilation into white society that the other Civilized Tribes did. They adopted white customs, manners, and dress in an effort to adapt to their changing surroundings.

During the era of Indian Removal, the Chickasaw were compensated financially for their lands. They were given $3 million for their tribal lands east of the Mississippi River. The tribe then used a portion of these funds to purchase land in Indian Territory which belonged to the Choctaw.

Today, the Chickasaw Nation has approximately 49,000 members. The tribe's headquarters are in Ada, Oklahoma.

Multiple Choice: *Select the choice that completes the statement or answers the question.*

1._____ Which of the following best explains why it is believed that the Chickasaw originally came from the western portion of the continent?
a. Oral histories suggest that their ancestors moved from that region.
b. Artifacts found by archaeologists contained a type of clay only found in western soil.
c. Many early Spanish explorers documented meeting Chickasaw tribesmen in New Mexico.
d. Geological evidence suggests that a flood in the western portion of the continent forced many tribes to migrate east.

2._____ Which of the following best summarizes the beliefs of Chickasaw and other Native American tribes?
a. Beliefs were passed down in a holy text. This text was strictly adhered to and was read only by tribal elders.
b. Beliefs were learned by memory at an early age. Chickasaw students attended many hours of school to learn all beliefs before they could join society.
c. Beliefs were passed down orally in the form of stories. These stories were usually about animals and had different meanings depending on the tribe.
d. The Chickasaw had no major belief system. Tribal elders determined issues of right and wrong on an independent basis.

3._____ Which evaluation best describes why the Chickasaw were polygamous?
a. Many Chickasaw women were unable to bear sons, so polygamy was necessary.
b. The Chickasaw were warlike and aggressive; their male population was constantly depleted.
c. Chickasaw males were gone for long periods of time on hunting expeditions. During these times, the wives depended on each other for survival.
d. Chickasaw women frequently died at an early age, creating the necessity for a man to take many wives.

4._____ Which of the following best summarizes the Chickasaw's first encounter with Europeans?
a. The Chickasaw greeted the Spaniards warmly and exchanged many goods with them.
b. The Chickasaw chased away the French, hoping that a show of force would prevent them from returning.
c. The Chickasaw were unexpectedly attacked by the English, and thousands died.
d. The Chickasaw had several disagreements with the Spaniards, which ended with the Spaniards being attacked.

5._____ Which of the following best describes what happened to the Chickasaw during the Indian Removal process?
a. The Chickasaw were rounded up at gunpoint and forced onto land in western Indian Territory.
b. The Chickasaw sold their lands for $3 million and purchased part of the Choctaw lands in Indian Territory.
c. The Chickasaw were promised all of western Kansas, but instead were forced to accept a small piece of land in eastern Indian Territory.
d. The Chickasaw fought a prolonged war with the US Army and were eventually allowed to remain on their tribal lands.

Guided Reading: *Fill in the blanks below to create complete sentences.*

1. The Chickasaw's ancestors lived in the Mississippi River Valley for _____ of years.

2. Tales related to creation, and other events deemed _____, were passed down orally in the form of stories.

3. In some cases, the male was required to ask _____ of the female before he could take another wife.

4. As white settlers moved into the southeastern portion of the continent throughout the 1700s, the Chickasaw grew more _____ to their presence.

5. Today, the Chickasaw Nation has approximately _____ members.

Vocabulary: *Match each word with its correct definition. Consider how the word is used in the lesson. This might help you define each term. Use a dictionary to help if necessary.*

a. originate
b. polygamy
c. perpetual

d. assimilation
e. compensation

6._____ continuing on forever; without end

7._____ an item of equal value that is given in exchange for something

8._____ the merging of cultural traits by previously distinct groups

9._____ the practice of having more than one wife at the same time

10._____ to begin or start; bring into being

Correct the Statement: *Each of the following sentences is false. Circle the incorrect word and write the word or phrase that makes the statement correct in the answer blank provided.*

11. The Chickasaw are a native tribe that once lived in the present-day states of Mississippi, Alabama, and Florida. _____.

12. Some historians suggest that the Chickasaw emerged as a tribe as late as the 1800s. _____.

13. There is a legend that states the Chickasaw rose up from a large earthwork mound called the Spiro Mound. _____.

14. In 1540, the Chickasaw were quite uncivilized, with their own laws and governmental system.

_____

15. The tribe adopted native customs, manners, and dress in an effort to adapt to their changing surroundings. _____.

Summarize: *Answer the following questions in the space provided. Attempt to respond in a complete sentence for each question. Be sure to use correct capitalization and punctuation.*

1. Who became the first European to encounter the Chickasaw in 1540?

2. What were the Chickasaw given as compensation for their tribal lands during the Indian Removal process?

3. When was the earthwork mound called Nanih Waiya most likely constructed?

4. Where did the Chickasaw once live? (In which present-day states?)

5. Why did the Chickasaw attack the Spaniards?

6. How were stories passed down amongst the Chickasaw?

Student Response: *Write a paragraph addressing the questions raised below. A thorough response should consist of three to five complete sentences.*

7. Why do you suppose animals played such a strong role in stories about Native American beliefs?

The Creek

One of the groups included amongst the Five Civilized Tribes was the Creek. Where did the Creek live? Were they always known by that name?

The Creek are descended from the Mississippian culture that existed for thousands of years in the Mississippi River Valley. The Mississippian culture was nearly wiped out by the arrival of Hernando de Soto. De Soto and his fellow Spaniards brought with them many diseases that the Native Americans had no immunity to. These diseases caused the collapse of the Mississippian culture. Those who survived these epidemics eventually regrouped as the Creek Confederacy.

The Creek are also known by the name Muscogee. This name was frequently used because of the common Muscogee language spoken in the region by several tribes. These tribes lived throughout the region of present-day Tennessee, Georgia, and Alabama.

In Creek society, the most important social unit was the clan (similar to a family). Clans were typically named after animals, such as the Bear Clan, Beaver Clan, Otter Clan, or Deer Clan. These clans arranged marriages, organized hunts, and punished lawbreakers. The village chief, or mico, was the leader of the community. The mico represented the village in negotiations with other villages and led warriors in battle. However, there were many others who assisted the mico. There were lesser chiefs, village elders, and a ranking warrior who all served the mico as advisers.

> *Words to watch for:*
>
> confederacy fervor
>
> purification rhetoric

There was also a village medicine man known as the Yahola. The Yahola officiated over religious rituals and purification ceremonies. He was also responsible for issuing the "black drink". Black drink was a substance made from Yaupon Holly and other various roots. It was only used during purification rituals because it induced vomiting (which was part of the purification process). Black drink was commonly used by many tribes all over the Southeast.

In the late 1700s, there was an effort made by the United States government to "civilize" the Creek. In 1796, President George Washington assigned Benjamin Hawkins as the General Superintendent of Indian Affairs for all the tribes south of the Ohio River. Hawkins personally assumed responsibility for assimilating the Creeks into the mainstream culture. He moved into Creek territory and began teaching proper farming techniques, as well as introducing them to Christianity and European methods of education.

In 1813, much of what Hawkins had worked to achieve was destroyed. A faction of Creek had joined the Shawnee chief Tecumseh in his fight against white settlers. Caught up in the fervor of his rhetoric, they chose to reject the adjustment to European American culture and fight back against encroachment.

This precipitated a civil war amongst the Creek, known as the Red Stick War. The Red Sticks were those who opposed white encroachment, while those who sought peaceful relations with the settlers became known as the White Sticks. The Red Stick War quickly became part of the larger War of 1812 that was being fought between the United States and Great Britain. The Red Sticks were eventually crushed by General Andrew Jackson at the Battle of Horseshoe Bend on March 27, 1814.

In the 1830s, the Creek Nation signed several removal treaties, just as the other civilized tribes did. The tribe ceded their lands east of the Mississippi River in exchange for lands in Indian Territory. They were then forcibly removed from their native lands.

Today, the Muscogee (Creek) Nation is a federally-recognized Indian Nation. Their headquarters can be found in Okmulgee, Oklahoma. There are approximately 71,500 members of the tribe.

Multiple Choice: *Select the choice that completes the statement or answers the question.*

1._____ Which of the following best describes what happened to the Mississippian culture?
a.   There was a major war between the Mississippian tribes and they were wiped out.
b.   The Mississippian tribes mutually agreed to disband and join other tribes.
c.   The Mississippian tribes were nearly wiped out by diseases they had no immunity to.
d.   There was a major disagreement over who should be the next leader, causing a split.

2._____ The Creek are also known by which of the following names?
a.   Iroquois   c.   Red Sticks
b.   Mississippi   d.   Muscogee

3._____ Which of the following correctly identifies the major responsibilities of the clan in Creek life?
a.   The clan arranged marriages, organized hunts, and punished lawbreakers.
b.   The clan represented the village in negotiations with other villages.
c.   The clan selected a representative who served as an adviser to the village chief.
d.   The clan had no major responsibilities and was merely an established tradition.

4._____ How did General Superintendent of Indian Affairs Benjamin Hawkins
            treat the Creek?
a.   He tricked them into signing removal treaties and then had the tribe forcibly removed
     from their native lands.
b.   He taught them farming techniques, as well as introducing them to Christianity and
     European methods of education.
c.   He forced them to build a home and then treated the Creek as if they were his slaves while
     he lived on Creek land.
d.   He dismissed all the Creek chiefs from their positions of leadership and named himself as
     the dictator of all Creek tribes.

5._____ Which of the following best summarizes the cause of the Red Stick War?
a.   This was a war between Creeks who had a strong disagreement about who should be the next leader of
     the Creek Nation.
b.   This was a war between the Creek Nation and the French, who were trying to claim Creek lands.
c.   This was a war between the Creek Nation and the Choctaw. Each tribe was claiming land in
     Mississippi belonged to them.
d.   This was a war between Creeks who opposed encroachment by settlers and those who hoped to
     negotiate with settlers peacefully.

Vocabulary: *Match each word with its correct definition. Consider how the word is used in the lesson.*
This might help you define each term. Use a dictionary to help if necessary.

a.   confederacy   d.   rhetoric
b.   purification   e.   encroach
c.   fervor

6._____ to free from contamination; to make clean

7._____ the effective use of language; the art of public speaking

8._____ a loose alliance of states in which the members keep most of their independence

9._____ great intensity of feeling or belief

10._____ to gradually intrude upon the rights or property of another

Guided Reading: *Fill in the blanks below to create complete sentences.*

1. The Mississippians who survived these epidemics of disease eventually regrouped as the _____ Confederacy.

2. The name Muscogee was frequently used because of the common Muscogee _____ spoken in the region by several tribes.

3. Clans were typically named after _____, such as the Bear Clan, Beaver Clan, Otter Clan, or Deer Clan.

4. The Yahola officiated over _____ rituals and purification ceremonies.

5. Today, the Muscogee (Creek) Nation is a federally-recognized Indian _____ with approximately 71,500 members.

Correct the Statement: *Each of the following sentences is false. Circle the incorrect word and write the word or phrase that makes the statement correct in the answer blank provided.*

6. The Mississippian culture was nearly wiped out by the arrival of Francisco Coronado. _____.

7. The village chief was also known as the Yahola. _____.

8. Black drink was a substance made from Yaupon Holly and other various chemicals. _____.

9. In 1796, President George Washington assigned Benjamin Hawkins as the General Superintendent of Indian Affairs for all the tribes north of the Ohio River.

_____.

10. Those who sought peaceful relations with the settlers became known as the Red Sticks. _____.

Summarize: *Answer the following questions in the space provided. Attempt to respond in a complete sentence for each question. Be sure to use correct capitalization and punctuation!*

1. Who was responsible for representing the village in negotiations with other villages?

2. What was another title for the village medicine man?

3. When did the Creek Nation sign several removal treaties?

4. Where were the Red Sticks eventually crushed?

5. Why was the black drink only used during purification ceremonies?

6. How did lesser chiefs, village elders, and the ranking warrior serve the mico?

Student Response: *Write a paragraph addressing the questions raised below. A thorough response should consist of three to five complete sentences.*

7. Why do you suppose the European Americans felt it was necessary to "civilize" the Native Americans?

The Seminole

The Seminole are the youngest of the Five Civilized Tribes. Where did the Seminole come from? Where are they now?

In the early 1700s, Creek Indians from the present-day states of Alabama, Georgia, and northern Florida began settling further south in Florida. These Creek eventually established their own tribe, which became known as the Seminole. The word "Seminole" is a corruption of the Spanish word "Cimarron" which means "runaway". Therefore, in a sense, the Seminole are runaways from the Creek tribe.

Over the course of time, African slaves escaping from Georgia joined the Seminole in Florida. These slaves intermingled with the Seminole and became a part of their tribe. They married Seminole and had children. Many African words worked their way into the Seminole language (a dialect of the Muscogee language).

One of the most important ceremonial traditions amongst the Seminole is the Green Corn Ceremony. This ceremony was practiced in some form by many different tribes throughout the Southeast, including the Creek and Cherokee. The Green Corn Ceremony, also known as Posketv, represents the coming of the new year and was celebrated in late June or early July. It was associated with the return of summer and the ripening of new corn. The Green Corn Ceremony was a celebration of the continued cycle of life.

In the early stages of European settlement of North America, the Seminole had friendly relations with both the Spanish and the British. However, in the early 1800s, tensions mounted quickly when the US Army began making frequent excursions into Florida (owned by Spain at the time) to recapture runaway slaves. This led to the First Seminole War, 1817-18, and Andrew Jackson's campaign against the Seminole. In 1819, the United States took possession of Florida following the passage of the Adams-Onis Treaty.

After the US gained control of Florida, land-hungry settlers began filtering into the new territory. Pressure mounted to remove the Seminole from the area. Just like the other Civilized Tribes, the Seminole were forcibly removed from their tribal lands. However, they did not leave without a fight. The Second Seminole War was fought by Osceola and his followers in an effort to maintain their lands. In the end, a large percentage of the Seminole were removed to Indian Territory, but many remained in Florida.

> *Words to watch for:*
>
> *intermingled   dialect*
>
> *ceremony   excursions*

Today, there are officially three Seminole Nations. The Seminole Nation of Oklahoma, the Seminole Tribe of Florida, and the Miccosukee Tribe of Indians of Florida are all federally-recognized and exist independent of each other. Collectively, there are more than 18,000 Seminole in the United States.

Multiple Choice: *Select the choice that completes the statement or answers the question.*

1._____ Which of the following correctly identifies the origin of the word "Seminole"?
a. Seminole is a corruption of the Creek word "Semiyola" which means "river people".
b. Seminole is a corruption of the Spanish word "Cimarron" which means "swamp people".
c. Seminole is a corruption of the Cherokee word "Samanella" which means "little people".
d. Seminole is a corruption of the Spanish word "Cimarron" which means "runaway".

2._____ Which of the following best summarizes how African slaves began to intermingle with the Seminole?
a. The Seminole purchased slaves from slave traders, just as their neighbors in Georgia did.
b. Slaves escaping from Georgia would intermarry with the tribe.
c. At some point in their distant past, the Seminole had journeyed to Africa.
d. The Seminole were introduced to slavery as part of their assimilation into European American culture.

3._____ Which of the following best explains the significance of the Green Corn Ceremony?
a. The ceremony represented the coming of the new year. It was associated with the return of summer and the ripening of the corn.
b. The ceremony represented the passing of the old year. It was associated with the return of fall and the harvesting of the corn.
c. The ceremony represented the return of new life and was associated with the coming of spring.
d. The ceremony represented the death of elders and was associated with the onset of winter.

4._____ Which of the following best explains what led to the First Seminole War in 1817-18?
a. The Seminole were fighting each other over who would be the next Seminole leader.
b. The US Army began making excursions into Florida, trying to recapture runaway slaves.
c. The US Army was attempting to remove the Seminole from their tribal lands.
d. The Seminole fought against the Creek in an effort to win their independence from them.

5._____ Which of the following best explains the purpose of the Second Seminole War?
a. The Seminole were fighting against the Creek in the Red Stick War.
b. The Seminole had allied themselves with the British during the War of 1812.
c. The Seminole were fighting to maintain possession of their tribal lands in Florida.
d. The Seminole were fighting a war of aggression against the Choctaw, attempting to take their lands.

Vocabulary: *Match each word with its correct definition. Consider how the word is used in the lesson. This might help you define each term. Use a dictionary to help if necessary.*

a. intermingle
b. dialect
c. ceremony
d. excursion
e. collectively

6._____ formed in a large group; the whole of something

7._____ a form of a language spoken in a particular geographic region

8._____ a formal religious or sacred observance

9._____ to mix between groups

10._____ a trip our outing to some place, usually with a specific purpose

Guided Reading: *Fill in the blanks below to create complete sentences.*

1. In the early 1700s, Creek Indians from the present-day states of Alabama, Georgia, and northern Florida began settling further south in _____.

2. Many African words worked their way into the Seminole language (a dialect of the _____ language).

3. The Green Corn Ceremony was practiced in some form by many different tribes throughout the Southeast, including the Creek and _____.

4. In the early stages of European settlement of North America, the Seminole had _____ relations with both the Spanish and the British.

5. Today, there are officially _____ Seminole Nations.

History Word Builder: *Match each historical term with its correct definition.*

a. Seminole
b. Green Corn Ceremony
c. Andrew Jackson
d. Adams-Onis
e. Osceola

6._____The treaty which allowed the United States to take possession of Florida.

7._____A corruption of the Spanish word "Cimarron" which means "runaway".

8._____Seminole leader who fought against the removal process in the 1830s.

9._____US officer who fought against the Seminole in the First Seminole War.

10._____Celebrates the coming of summer and the ripening of the corn.

Summarize: *Answer the following questions in the space provided. Attempt to respond in a complete sentence for each question. Be sure to use correct capitalization and punctuation!*

1. Who intermingled and married into the Seminole tribe?

2. What are the names of the three federally-recognized Seminole nations?

3. When did the US take possession of Florida?

4. Where was the Seminole tribe located? (Which state?)

5. Why did pressure begin to mount to remove the Seminole from their lands?

6. How were Seminole relations with the Spanish and British in the early days of European settlement?

Student Response: *Write a paragraph addressing the questions raised below. A thorough response should consist of three to five complete sentences.*

7. Why do you suppose that ceremonies such as the Green Corn Ceremony were common amongst many Native American tribes and not just one?

The Choctaw, Chickasaw, and Creek lived throughout the southern portion of the United States. Utilize a map of the United States, or internet resources, to help you locate and label the following places mentioned in this unit:

Rivers should be drawn in and labeled. Cities should be labeled with a •

Tennessee	Louisiana	Mississippi	Alabama
Florida	Mississippi River	Ada, Oklahoma	Okmulgee, Oklahoma

Color each labeled state a different color.

The Five Civilized Tribes: Post Assessment

Vocabulary: *Match each word with its correct definition.*

a. confederacy   e. migration
b. assimilation   f. autonomy
c. epidemic   g. polygamy
d. matrilineal   h. dialect

1._____ the merging of cultural traits by previously distinct groups

2._____ the practice of having more than one wife at the same time

3._____ a societal structure based on the female's family line

4._____ a loose alliance of states in which the members keep most of their independence

5._____ self-governing; independent

6._____ the process of a large group of people moving from one place to another

7._____ a disease that affects many people at the same time

8._____ a form of a language spoken in a particular geographic region

Completion: *Fill in the blanks below to create complete sentences.*

lacrosse   traditional   confederation
tattooed   Tuskaloosa   Civilized

9. The earliest white settlers stated that the Cherokee had heavily-painted and
_____ skin.

10. The adoption of European customs is what led to the Cherokee and other tribes becoming known as the _____ Tribes.

11. The Cherokee were a loose _____, with each group having autonomy over their own village.

12. The full-bloods were more _____ and hoped to hold on to the old ways and customs.

13. Hernando de Soto took Chief _____ hostage and made many demands. In retaliation, the Choctaw attacked de Soto.

14. Stickball was eventually altered by Europeans and is still played today in the form of
_____.

Completion: *Fill in the blanks below to create complete sentences.*

religious   creation   Mississippi
Creek   Green Corn   animals

15. The Chickasaw's ancestors lived in the _____ River Valley for thousands of years.

16. Tales related to _____, and other events deemed important, were passed down orally in the form of stories.

17. The Mississippians who survived the epidemics of disease eventually regrouped as the _____ Confederacy.

18. Clans were typically named after _____, such as the Bear Clan, Beaver Clan, Otter Clan, or Deer Clan.

19. The Yahola officiated over _____ rituals and purification ceremonies.

20. The _____ Ceremony was practiced in some form by many different tribes throughout the Southeast, including the Creek and Cherokee.

Multiple Choice: *Select the choice that completes the statement or answers the question.*

21._____ Which famous explorer was the first to contact several of the Five Civilized Tribes?
a. Francisco Coronado   c. Hernando de Soto
b. Bernard de LaHarpe   d. Ponce de Leon

22._____ Which of the following most accurately reflects why little is known about the Cherokee prior to the arrival of European settlers?
a. The Cherokee are very secretive and do not tell outsiders about their tribal history.
b. Most of the Cherokee records from that time period were lost in a great fire.
c. The Cherokee, like other Native American tribes, did not keep written records.
d. The Cherokee tribe did not exist until very recently.

23._____ Which of the following best describes the clothing worn by the Cherokee when they first encountered European explorers?
a. Many Cherokee already dressed in the European fashions of the day.
b. They wore bits of cloth and large garments that hung over the entire body.
c. Most wore broad hats and breastplates made of solid gold.
d. They wore shoes carved from wood and buffalo hide clothing.

24._____ Which of the following properly identifies the two competing groups of Cherokee during the Indian Removal process?
a. The white and the red   c. The full-bloods and the mixed-bloods
b. The traditionalists and the progressives   d. The Bear Party and the Moose Party

25._____ Which of the following best summarizes George Washington's approach to dealing with the Native American way of life?
a. Washington hoped to move Native Americans west so that their way of life would not be disrupted.
b. Washington declared war with the intention of eradicating natives from North America.
c. Washington took them as slaves and sold thousands of Native Americans into slavery in Europe.
d. Washington assigned government agents to live amongst the tribes and teach them how to live like European Americans.

26._____ Which of the following best describes a matrilineal society?
a. A society in which the male is the head of the household, and all inheritance is passed through the male's family.
b. A society in which the female is the head of the household, and all inheritance is passed through the female's family.
c. A society in which each male is allowed to marry as many wives as he would like, as long as he is capable of providing for them.
d. A society in which the female is allowed to marry as many husbands as she would like, as long as she is capable of taking care of them all.

27._____ Which of the following best explains why Pushmataha refused to fight with Tecumseh against the United States?
a. Pushmataha argued that the Choctaw had always had good relations with the white man.
b. Pushmataha was a pacifist and refused to engage in any type of violence.
c. Pushmataha had already signed an agreement with the government which made him fabulously wealthy.
d. Pushmataha had seen too many wars in his lifetime and refused to start another.

28._____ Which of the following best summarizes the Treaty of Doak's Stand?
a. The Choctaw agreed to cease all hostilities against the US government.
b. The Choctaw agreed to pay the United States $3 million to continue living on their tribal lands.
c. The Choctaw agreed to cede nearly half of their tribal lands to the United States.
d. The Choctaw agreed to join the United States and enter the Union as the state of Mississippi.

29._____ Which of the following best summarizes the beliefs of Chickasaw and other Native American tribes?
a. Beliefs were passed down in a holy text. This text was strictly adhered to and was read only by tribal elders.
b. Beliefs were learned by memory at an early age. Chickasaw students attended many hours of school to learn all beliefs before they could join society.
c. Beliefs were passed down orally in the form of stories. These stories were usually about animals and had different meanings depending on the tribe.
d. The Chickasaw had no major belief system. Tribal elders determined issues of right and wrong on an independent basis.

30._____ Which evaluation best describes why the Chickasaw were polygamous?
a. Many Chickasaw women were unable to bear sons, so polygamy was necessary.
b. The Chickasaw were warlike and aggressive; their male population was constantly depleted.
c. Chickasaw males were gone for long periods of time on hunting expeditions. During these times, the wives depended on each other for survival.
d. Chickasaw women frequently died at an early age, creating the necessity for a man to take many wives.

31._____ Which of the following best summarizes the Chickasaw's first encounter
with Europeans?
a. The Chickasaw greeted the Spaniards warmly and exchanged many goods with them.
b. The Chickasaw chased away the French, hoping that a show of force would prevent them
from returning.
c. The Chickasaw were unexpectedly attacked by the English, and thousands died.
d. The Chickasaw had several disagreements with the Spaniards, which ended with the
Spaniards being attacked.

32._____ Which of the following best describes what happened to the Mississippian culture?
a. There was a major war between the Mississippian tribes and they were wiped out.
b. The Mississippian tribes mutually agreed to disband and join other tribes.
c. The Mississippian tribes were nearly wiped out by diseases they had no immunity to.
d. There was a major disagreement over who should be the next leader, causing a split.

33._____ The Creek are also known by which of the following names?
a. Iroquois   c. Red Sticks
b. Mississippi   d. Muscogee

34._____ In Creek society, the village chief was known by what title?
a. chief   c. president
b. mico   d. medicine man

35._____ Which of the following best summarizes the cause of the Red Stick War?
a. This was a war between Creeks who had a strong disagreement about who should be the next
leader of the Creek Nation.
b. This was a war between the Creek Nation and the French, who were trying to claim Creek lands.
c. This was a war between the Creek Nation and the Choctaw. Each tribe was claiming land in
Mississippi belonged to them.
d. This was a war between Creeks who opposed encroachment by settlers and those who hoped to
negotiate with settlers peacefully.

36._____ The Red Stick War came to an end at which famous battle?
a. Battle of New Orleans   c. Battle of Horseshoe Bend
b. Battle of Gettysburg   d. Battle of Yorktown

37._____ The Seminole tribe was almost exclusively located in which state?
a. Mississippi   c. Alabama
b. Georgia   d. Florida

38._____ Which of the following best summarizes how African slaves began to intermingle
with the Seminole?
a. The Seminole purchased slaves from slave traders, just as their neighbors in Georgia did.
b. Slaves escaping from Georgia would intermarry with the tribe.
c. At some point in their distant past, the Seminole had journeyed to Africa.
d. The Seminole were introduced to slavery as part of their assimilation into European
American culture.

39._____ Which of the following best explains the significance of the Green Corn Ceremony?
a. The ceremony represented the coming of the new year. It was associated with the return of summer and the ripening of the corn.
b. The ceremony represented the passing of the old year. It was associated with the return of fall and the harvesting of the corn.
c. The ceremony represented the return of new life and was associated with the coming of spring.
d. The ceremony represented the death of elders and was associated with the onset of winter.

40._____ Which of the following best explains what led to the First Seminole War in 1817-18?
a. The Seminole were fighting each other over who would be the next Seminole leader.
b. The US Army began making excursions into Florida, trying to recapture runaway slaves.
c. The US Army was attempting to remove the Seminole from their tribal lands.
d. The Seminole fought against the Creek in an effort to win their independence from them.

Creek Removal

The process known as "Indian Removal" which occurred in the 1830s is easily one of the darkest chapters in the history of the United States. Why did this process occur? Which tribes did it involve?

In the early 1800s, the United States was growing at a rapid pace. Unfortunately, as the population continued to expand, land was becoming scarce. Eager white settlers began desiring lands which belonged to Native Americans. In the South, lands owned by the Creek, Choctaw, Chickasaw, Cherokee, and Seminole tribes were in high demand. These regions contained quality farmland and were potentially rich in minerals.

William McIntosh

The Creek Nation had made it a capital offense to sign a treaty which gave Creek lands to the United States. However, on February 12, 1825, William McIntosh and several other Creek chiefs signed the Treaty of Indian Springs. This treaty ceded all the Creek lands in Georgia to the United States for $200,000. McIntosh signed the treaty because, according to the conditions of the treaty, he would personally receive a large portion of this money. For signing the Treaty of Indian Springs, McIntosh was executed by the tribe. Another Creek chief was also put to death.

The Creek appealed to the government, claiming that the treaty was not legitimate because McIntosh did not represent the entire tribe. The government agreed and annulled the treaty. This became one of the rare occasions when the U.S. government annulled such a treaty that had been ratified.

In 1830, the United States Congress passed the Indian Removal Act. This act gave the government official authority to negotiate with the Native Americans for their tribal land. With the passage of this law, the official policy of the United States became removing Native Americans from their eastern lands and into Indian Territory west of Mississippi River.

More than 20,000 Creeks still lived in the state of Alabama. The state made many efforts to try and make life uncomfortable for the Creeks. The state legislature attempted to abolish the tribal government and force the Creeks to abide by state laws. Those hoping to obtain Creek land began encroaching on Creek property and harassing Creek land owners. When the Creek attempted to defend themselves, it was declared an uprising.

Words to watch for:

rapid   legitimate

annulled infested

General Winfield Scott was ordered to bring an end to the "Creek rebellion" and move the Creek west of the Mississippi River by force. The Creeks were rounded up and forced into heavily-guarded, rat-infested camps. They were bound in shackles and chains and forced to march from Alabama to their new home in Indian Territory. By 1837, more than 15,000 Creeks had arrived at Fort Gibson in Indian Territory. However, it is estimated that more than 3,000 who began the trip did not survive. Most of those who perished were small children and the elderly.

Once the Creek had arrived in Indian Territory, life was not much better. Homes had to be constructed and ground had to be cleared. Fields were being plowed for the first time. Prior to their first harvest, a flood wiped out their crops, destroyed many newly built homes, and carried away much of the livestock. As a result, the Creek faced a severe food shortage during the first winter in their new home. This brought even more death to the tribe. It has been speculated that between the removal process and the difficulties of their first year in Indian Territory, more than 40% of the total Creek population perished.

Multiple Choice: *Select the choice that completes the statement or answers the question.*

1._____ Which of the following best explains why land owned by the Five Civilized Tribes was in high demand amongst white settlers?
a. All of their tribal lands were near the coast. This land was highly valuable for overseas trading.
b. All of their tribal lands were near major rivers. These waterways were important for shipping, as well as sources of freshwater.
c. The tribal lands were known to be in spots that would not be severely impacted by natural disasters such as tornadoes and hurricanes.
d. Quality farmland that was rich in minerals was becoming increasingly scarce as more settlers moved into the region.

2._____ Which of the following best summarizes what happened to William McIntosh for signing the Treaty of Indian Springs?
a. He was executed by the tribe.
b. He was removed from his position as chief.
c. He was excommunicated from the tribe.
d. He was praised as one of the greatest Creek chiefs in history.

3._____ Which of the following best describes the significance of the Indian Removal Act of 1830?
a. The United States abandoned its efforts to remove Native Americans from their lands and allowed the tribes live in peace.
b. The official policy of the United States became the assimilation of Native Americans into mainstream culture.
c. The official policy of the United States became removing Native Americans from their tribal lands and into Indian Territory.
d. The United States began its effort to locate a piece of land in South America where Native Americans could live in peace.

4._____ Which of the following statements is not true?
a. Creeks were rounded up and forced into heavily-guarded, rat-infested camps.
b. Creeks were bound in shackles and chains and forced to march to Indian Territory.
c. By 1837, more than 150,000 Creeks had arrived at Fort Gibson in Indian Territory.
d. The journey to Indian Territory was hardest on small children and the elderly.

5._____ Which of the following was *not* one of the problems faced by the Creek after they arrived in Indian Territory?
a. An unexpected heat wave made conditions miserable.
b. Fields were being plowed for the first time.
c. A flood wiped out their first harvest.
d. Many of their new homes were destroyed by flood.

Vocabulary: *Match each word with its correct definition. Consider how the word is used in the lesson. This might help you define each term. Use a dictionary to help if necessary.*

a. rapid
b. capital offense
c. legitimate

d. annul
e. infest

1._____ in accordance with the law; legal

2._____ occurring within a short period of time; quick

3._____ overrun with dangerously large numbers

4._____ to make void, abolish, or cancel

5._____ a crime which is punishable by death

Guided Reading: *Fill in the blanks below to create complete sentences.*

6. In the early 1800s, eager white settlers began desiring lands which belonged to

_____.

7. The Treaty of Indian Springs ceded all the Creek lands in _____ to the United States for $200,000.

8. The Creek appealed to the _____, claiming that the Treaty of Indian Springs was not legitimate.

9. The Alabama state legislature attempted to abolish the _____ government and force the Creeks to abide by state laws.

10. It is estimated that more than _____ who attempted to make the trip to Indian Territory perished in the process.

History Word Builder: *Match each historical term with its correct definition.*

a. Treaty of Indian Springs
b. William McIntosh
c. Indian Removal Act of 1830

d. Winfield Scott
e. Fort Gibson

11._____ General who was responsible for moving the Creek west of the Mississippi River.

12._____ The arrival point in Indian Territory for the Creek and many other tribes.

13._____ A Creek removal treaty that was annulled by the US government.

14._____ A law which gave the US government the authority to negotiate with Native American tribes for their lands.

15._____ A Creek chief who signed the Treaty of Indian Springs.

Summarize: *Answer the following questions in the space provided. Attempt to respond in a complete sentence for each question. Be sure to use correct capitalization and punctuation!*

1. Who was responsible for moving the Creek west of the Mississippi River?

2. What was Alabama's reason for abolishing the tribal government and forcing the Creek to abide by state laws?

3. When was the Indian Removal Act passed?

4. According to the Indian Removal Act, where were the Native Americans going to be moved to?

5. Why did William McIntosh sign the Treaty of Indian Springs?

6. How were the Creek able to argue that the Treaty of Indian Springs wasn't legitimate?

Student Response: *Write a paragraph addressing the questions raised below. A thorough response should consist of three to five complete sentences.*

7. Consider the position of William McIntosh. Would you sign a treaty, knowing you would become quite wealthy, but also knowing that you might be executed for signing? Why or why not? Explain your answer as thoroughly as possible.

Choctaw and Chickasaw Removal

The Choctaw and Chickasaw faced the same removal process as the other Civilized Tribes. How difficult was this process? How did the two tribes end up together?

The Choctaw lived in Alabama, Mississippi, and Louisiana. Starting in 1801, a series of treaties had reduced the Choctaw lands to 11,000,000 acres. Finally, in 1831, the Choctaw signed the Treaty of Dancing Rabbit Creek. Under the terms of this treaty, the Choctaw agreed to forfeit their remaining lands east of the Mississippi River in exchange for land in Indian Territory.

> *Words to watch for:*
>
> *forfeit   rations*
>
> *harassment merged*

The removal of the Choctaw was planned to begin in 1831 and end in 1833. The conditions the tribe faced were horrible, including sleet, snow, and floods. Efforts to move the tribe with wagons failed because of the flood conditions, so instead, they boarded five steamboats. Unfortunately, after traveling about 60 miles, the river froze over and they were unable to continue for weeks.

The Trail of Tears

They were forced to survive on food rations that included a handful of corn, a turnip, and two cups of water a day. Finally, forty wagons were sent to take them the rest of the way. Another group of Choctaw became lost in the swamps and were never seen again.

Almost 17,000 Choctaw eventually arrived in Indian Territory. More than 2,500 had died during their travels. At one point, a Choctaw chief stated that their journey had been "a trail of tears". This phrase eventually came to be used to describe the relocation of all the Civilized Tribes to Indian Territory.

Some Choctaw were allowed to remain in Mississippi (as part of the conditions of the Treaty of Dancing Rabbit Creek). However, these Choctaw faced harassment and intimidation from white settlers. Their homes were burned and their livestock was destroyed in effort to make their lives so miserable that they would want to leave. Most refused to be intimidated.

The Chickasaw removal was handled in a different manner. Instead of being given land in Indian Territory, the Chickasaw were given monetary compensation for their lands. The Chickasaw turned over their lands in Mississippi, Alabama, and Tennessee in exchange for $3 million. The tribe then paid the Choctaw $530,000 for the westernmost portion of their land in Indian Territory.

The Chickasaw removal was less difficult than the other tribes for multiple reasons. First, it was largely voluntary, with the members of the tribe gathering and organizing their belongings and livestock prior to the move. Also, they were traveling along established routes that had already been used by the earlier tribes. Finally, the region the Chickasaw were moving to had already been settled by the Choctaw. Once the Chickasaw arrived in Indian Territory, they merged together in a community with the Choctaw Nation.

Multiple Choice: *Select the choice that completes the statement or answers the question.*

1._____ Which of the following best summarizes the terms of the Treaty of
Dancing Rabbit Creek?
a. The Choctaw agreed to end hostilities between themselves and the United States government.
b. The Chickasaw agreed to merge with the Choctaw, officially uniting the two tribes.
c. The Choctaw agreed to forfeit lands east of the Mississippi River in exchange for lands in
Indian Territory.
d. The Choctaw agreed to bring an end to their long-standing war against the Creek Nation and allow
Creeks to pass through their lands.

2._____ Which of the following statements regarding the Choctaw removal is inaccurate?
a. The conditions were horrible and included sleet, snow, and floods.
b. A majority of the journey was made by traveling on steamboats.
c. They were forced to survive on a handful of corn, a turnip, and two cups of water a day.
d. One group of Choctaw became lost in the swamps and was never seen again.

3._____ Which of the following well-known phrases came from the Choctaw
removal process?
a. "I will fight no more, forever"   c. "proud to live, proud to die"
b. "a river of dreams"   d. "a trail of tears"

4._____ Which of the following most accurately describes how the Choctaw who remained
in Mississippi were treated?
a. They were treated warmly and encouraged to assimilate into mainstream culture.
b. They were harassed and intimidated in the hopes that they would decide to leave.
c. They were given autonomy and allowed to govern their lands as they saw fit.
d. They were isolated from society and forced to live on reservations.

5._____ Which of the following is *not* one of the reasons why the Chickasaw removal
was less difficult?
a. The Chickasaw removal was controlled by the US government.
b. The Chickasaw were traveling over already established routes.
c. The Chickasaw were allowed to gather and organize their belongings prior to the move.
d. The Chickasaw were moving to a region that had already been settled by the Choctaw.

Vocabulary: *Match each word with its correct definition. Consider how the word is used in the lesson.*
This might help you define each term. Use a dictionary to help if necessary.

a. forfeit   d. monetary
b. rations   e. merge
c. harassment

6._____ a fixed amount of food or other provisions

7._____ to give up, surrender, or relinquish

8._____ to combine or blend together

9._____ pertaining to money

10._____ to trouble or torment with continuous attacks

Name_____

Guided Reading: *Fill in the blanks below to create complete sentences.*

1. Starting in 1801, a series of _____ had reduced the Choctaw lands to 11,000,000 acres.

2. The conditions during the Choctaw removal were horrible and included sleet, _____, and floods.

3. Efforts to move the tribe with wagons failed because of the _____ conditions.

4. Moving by steamboat was unsuccessful because the river _____ over.

5. Almost 17,000 Choctaw eventually arrived in _____.

6. More than _____ Choctaw had died during their travels.

7. Some Choctaw were allowed to remain in _____.

8. The Choctaw who remained in Mississippi had their homes burned and their _____ destroyed.

9. The _____ turned over their lands in Mississippi, Alabama, and Tennessee in exchange for $3 million.

10. The Chickasaw then paid the _____ $530,000 for the westernmost portion of Choctaw land in Indian Territory.

Summarize: *Answer the following questions in the space provided. Attempt to respond in a complete sentence for each question. Be sure to use correct capitalization and punctuation!*

1. Who did the Chickasaw purchase land from in Indian Territory?

2. What was the name of the treaty the Choctaw signed in 1831?

3. When was the Choctaw removal supposed to occur?

4. Where were the Choctaw and Chickasaw moved to?

5. Why were the Choctaw homes burned?

6. How much did the government pay for Chickasaw tribal lands?

Student Response: *Write a paragraph addressing the questions raised below. A thorough response should consist of three to five complete sentences.*

7. Why do you suppose the Chickasaw were willing to leave their tribal lands in the manner they did?

Cherokee Nation v. Georgia (1831) & Worcester v. Georgia (1832)

In the 1830s, the Cherokee Nation and many other Native American tribes fought to keep their tribal lands in the southeastern United States. What were some of the Supreme Court cases that decided this issue?

The Cherokee Nation had lived in what is now Georgia for hundreds of years. In the year 1800, the Cherokee still owned quite a bit of land in Georgia, as well as Tennessee, North Carolina, and Alabama. By the early 1820s, white citizens in Georgia were clamoring for the Cherokee lands. The land was considered valuable because it was believed to contain gold.

Words to watch for:
tribal   negotiate
obtain   intention

In December of 1828, the Georgia state legislature began passing several laws, stripping the Cherokee of their rights. Their intention was to force the Cherokee out of Georgia. The Principal Chief of the Cherokee, John Ross, attempted to negotiate with the federal government. However, after the negotiations failed, the only remaining course of action was to bring their case to court.

Cherokee Nation v. Georgia was heard by the Supreme Court on March 18, 1831. While the Court did hear the case, they eventually determined that they could not make a ruling. They came to this conclusion on the basis that the Cherokee Nation was neither a foreign nation, nor were they American citizens. The Cherokee were deemed to be a "domestic dependent nation" and Chief Justice John Marshall suggested that "the relationship of the tribes to the United States resembles that of a ward to its guardian."

Amongst the laws passed by the state of Georgia was a measure that stated any American citizen living amongst the Cherokee had to obtain a license to live on Cherokee lands. Several Christian missionaries living with the Cherokee refused to comply with this law. One of those missionaries was Samuel Worcester. For violating the law, he was arrested and sentenced to four years of hard labor.

Since Samuel Worcester was a U.S. citizen, he could have a case heard in the Supreme Court. *Worcester v. Georgia* was heard in February of 1832. The Court ruled that the Cherokee Nation was a distinct community with its own government, and therefore the state of Georgia had no right to pass laws against it. This meant that Samuel Worcester should not have needed to obtain a license to live in Cherokee land and should be released.

Samuel Worcester

Chief Justice John Marshall's majority opinion stated that it was the federal government's responsibility to negotiate with the Native American tribes and *not* the responsibility of the states.

The ruling was controversial from the moment it was made. Even President Andrew Jackson is famously quoted as stating, "John Marshall's made his decision; now let him enforce it." While Jackson never spoke or wrote these actual words, his opinion was clear. He had no intention of preventing the state of Georgia from continuing its efforts against the Cherokee Nation.

While *Worcester v. Georgia* slowed the process, it did not succeed in keeping Georgia citizens from taking Cherokee lands. The end result became known as the Trail of Tears, which saw the forced relocation of more than 15,000 Cherokee to the present-day state of Oklahoma.

Multiple Choice: *Select the choice that completes the statement or answers the question.*

1._____ Why did Georgia citizens want Cherokee lands?
a.   It was considered the best farmland in the country.
b.   It was believed to contain gold.
c.   It was valuable ground which had oil underneath it.
d.   It was oceanfront property which was valuable for building vacation homes.

2._____ Why did the Supreme Court decide that it could not make a ruling in
          Cherokee Nation v. Georgia?
a.   The Cherokee had not filed the proper paperwork, so their claim was invalid.
b.   The state of Georgia had already negotiated a binding contract with the Cherokee.
c.   The Supreme Court could only rule on cases involving two different states.
d.   The Cherokee Nation was neither an independent nation nor were they citizens of the U.S.

3._____ Which of these most accurately describes the law Georgia passed in an effort to make life
          difficult for the Cherokee?
a.   Any U.S. citizen living on Cherokee lands had to apply for a license to do so.
b.   No citizen of the Cherokee Nation could apply for employment in the state of Georgia.
c.   All Cherokee were to report to internment camps and remain there until further notice.
d.   The Cherokee were subject to much higher rates of taxation than white citizens.

4._____ Who was Samuel Worcester?
a.   He was the highest ranking Chief of the Cherokee Nation.
b.   He was the US ambassador who negotiated with the Cherokee.
c.   He was a missionary who refused to get a license to live on Cherokee lands.
d.   He was a gold prospector who fought to live on Cherokee lands.

5._____ In *Worcester v. Georgia*, the Supreme Court ruled which of the following?
a.   The Court ruled that Georgia must return all lands to the Cherokee and pay them
     reparations for the wrongs committed.
b.   The Court ruled that the state of Georgia was perfectly within its rights to force the
     Cherokee from their lands.
c.   The Court ruled that Worcester could not have a case heard in court because he was not a
     US citizen.
d.   The Court ruled that it was the federal government's responsibility to negotiate with
     Native American tribes.

TRUE/FALSE: *Indicate whether the statement is true or false. If the statement is false,*
write the correct word or phrase in the space provided to make the statement true.

6._____ The Cherokee still owned land in Georgia, as well as Tennessee, North Carolina, and
          <u>Pennsylvania</u>. _____

7._____ The land was considered valuable because it was believed to contain <u>silver</u>.
          _____

8._____ *Worcester v. Georgia* was heard by the Supreme Court on March 18, 1831.
          _____

9._____ Since <u>Samuel Worcester</u> was a citizen of the United States, he could have a case heard in the
          Supreme Court. _____

10._____President Andrew Jackson had no intention of preventing the state of Georgia from continuing
          its efforts against the <u>Choctaw Nation</u>. _____

Guided Reading: *Fill in the blanks below to create complete sentences.*

1. The Cherokee Nation had lived in what is now _____ for hundreds of years.

2. The Georgia state legislature began passing several laws, stripping the Cherokee of their _____.

3. The Georgia state legislature's intention with these laws was to force the _____ out of Georgia.

4. The Principal Chief of the Cherokee, _____, attempted to negotiate with the federal government.

5. The Cherokee were deemed to be a "_____ nation".

6. Chief Justice John Marshall suggested that "the relationship of the tribes to the United States resembles that of a ward to its _____."

7. In *Worcester v. Georgia*, the Supreme Court ruled that the Cherokee Nation was a distinct community with its own _____, and therefore the state of Georgia had no right to pass laws against it.

8. Chief Justice John Marshall's majority opinion stated that it was the federal government's responsibility to _____ with the Native American tribes, *not* the state's responsibility.

9. President _____ is famously quoted as stating, "John Marshall's made his decision; now let him enforce it."

10. The forced relocation of more than 15,000 Cherokee to the present-day state of Oklahoma is known as _____.

Vocabulary Check: *Select the option that best identifies the use of the underlined word.*

1._____ In the first paragraph, the word <u>tribal</u> implies
a. A phial of Ancient Greece.
b. Belonging to a particular ethnic group or culture.
c. A group of people sharing an occupation.
d. Including more than one group or nationality.

2._____ "Their <u>intention</u> was to force the Cherokee out of Georgia." The word intention is used to mean
a. Movement in time; duration.
b. Onward movement in a particular direction.
c. To move swiftly through or over.
d. An aim that guides action; an objective.

3._____ In the third paragraph, the word <u>negotiate</u> means
a. To succeed in accomplishing or managing.
b. To transfer title or ownership to.
c. To confer with another or others in order to come to terms or reach an agreement.
d. Coping with a stressful situation.

4._____ "While the Court did hear the case, they eventually <u>determined</u> that they could not make a ruling." In the previous sentence, the word determined means
a. To end or decide, as by judicial action.
b. To limit in scope or extent.
c. Marked by or showing determination; resolute.
d. Within, allowed by, or sanctioned by the law; lawful.

5._____ In the fifth paragraph, the word <u>obtain</u> means
a. To be established, accepted, or customary.
b. A giving of funds for a specific purpose.
c. To gain possession of as the result of planning or endeavor; acquire.
d. The term or duration of a contract.

Student Response: *Please respond to the questions raised below. A thorough response should be a paragraph of at least three to five complete sentences.*

6. In *Worcester v. Georgia* you read that the Supreme Court made a ruling that seemed to favor the Cherokee Nation over the state of Georgia, but President Andrew Jackson chose to ignore it. Do you believe that the Supreme Court should have some kind of enforcement power over the other branches of government?

Cherokee Removal

One of the most tragic events to occur in American history has become known as the Trail of Tears? What was the Trail of Tears? Who was affected by it?

The Cherokee lived in parts of Georgia, Alabama, and Tennessee, as well as portions of North and South Carolina. By the 1820s, the tribe had become quite prosperous. They owned plantations, grain mills, lumber mills, and many other successful businesses. This success led to a fair amount of resentment amongst some of their white neighbors who were not as well off. This jealousy only increased with the discovery of gold on Cherokee lands in 1828.

The state of Georgia began passing several laws which were designed to make life miserable for the Cherokee. This was done in an effort to convince the Cherokee to leave. The Cherokee fought these laws in court, taking two different cases all the way to the Supreme Court. _The Cherokee Nation v. Georgia_ was thrown out by the high court, but _Worcester v. Georgia_ was decided in favor of the Cherokee. Despite this court decision, Georgia proceeded with their plans to remove the Cherokee from their native lands.

In 1835, the Treaty of New Echota was signed by several Cherokee leaders, including Major Ridge, John Ridge, and Elias Boudinot. The treaty required the Cherokee Nation to cede all of its land in the Southeast and move to Indian Territory. Some Cherokee made the move to Indian Territory peacefully. However, most of the tribe refused to leave and continued to fight for their lands.

The fight came to an end in 1838 when the remaining Cherokee were forcefully removed. 7,000 soldiers, led by General Winfield Scott, rounded up those who remained in Georgia. Families had their evening meals interrupted by troops with rifles and bayonets bursting through their door. Men were taken while plowing their land, and children were snatched up as they played in fields. The smallest cabins and even caves were searched to find every last Cherokee who might have been attempting to hide. Homes were looted and burned, and herds of livestock were seized.

The Cherokee were then forced to march on foot from Georgia and Tennessee to Indian Territory, and the journey was incredibly difficult. A large portion of the trip took place during winter, and most did not have shoes or blankets. There was very little food, and in many cases what was provided to them was already rotten. There were major outbreaks of diseases, such as cholera, and death rates were high. This journey to Indian Territory became known as the Trail of Tears. The trail's various routes measure more than 2,200 miles and cross through portions of nine states.

Words to watch for:

tragic ceded

looted cholera

As the process continued, the principal chief of the Cherokee, John Ross, convinced those in charge to allow him to oversee the removal. From that point on, things did improve slightly, but it was still extremely difficult.

When they arrived in Indian Territory, it was not a happy reunion between those who had left after the signing of the Treaty of New Echota and those who had suffered on the Trail of Tears. Ross believed that those who had signed the treaty were traitors. As a result, Major Ridge, John Ridge, and Elias Boudinot were executed.

The impact that the Trail of Tears had on the Cherokee can never be fully grasped. It is estimated that over 4,000 died during the journey to Indian Territory. Today, the trail is recognized as a National Historic Trail, and the Cherokee work diligently to ensure that the event will never be forgotten.

Multiple Choice: *Select the choice that completes the statement or answers the question.*

1._____ Which of the following best summarizes Cherokee life during the 1820s?
a.   The Cherokee were extremely poor and survived by subsistence farming, eating what they grew.
b.   The Cherokee owned plantations, lumber mills, grain mills, and many other successful businesses.
c.   The Cherokee lived in huts, wore little clothing, had heavily-tattooed skin, and hunted for food.
d.   The Cherokee were coastal fisherman who depended on daily catches to provide food for their village.

2._____ Which of the following best describes the laws that the state of Georgia was passing?
a.   The laws were designed to make life miserable for the Cherokee and convince them to leave.
b.   The laws were designed to make life easier for the Cherokee and convince them to stay.
c.   The laws were designed to help the Cherokee preserve their traditional ways of life.
d.   The laws were designed to help the Cherokee assimilate into mainstream culture.

3._____ Which of the following is most significant about the Treaty of New Echota?
a.   The treaty was signed by Major Ridge, John Ridge, and Elias Boudinot.
b.   This was the first removal treaty signed by any of the Five Civilized Tribes.
c.   This was the last of the major removal treaties signed by the Five Civilized Tribes.
d.   The treaty required the Cherokee Nation to cede all of its lands in the Southeast.

4._____ Which of the following best summarizes the Cherokee journey on the Trail of Tears?
a.   Most of the journey was conducted with wagons or on horseback. It was largely a smooth transition from Georgia to Indian Territory.
b.   The Cherokee were rounded up and packed into trains. They were then shipped hundreds of miles to Indian Territory.
c.   Most of the journey was on foot and during winter. Outbreaks of diseases, lack of food, and the harsh conditions resulted in thousands of deaths.
d.   The Cherokee traveled by boat, through the Gulf of Mexico and up the Mississippi and Arkansas Rivers to arrive in Indian Territory.

5._____ Which of the following best explains what happened to those who signed the
Treaty of New Echota?
a.   Those who signed the treaty were viewed as heroes and became the new leaders of the Cherokee.
b.   Those who signed the treaty were viewed as traitors and executed.
c.   Those who signed the treaty had their titles stripped from them and were forced to move out of the tribe.
d.   Those who signed the treaty were forced to make a public apology to other tribal members.

Vocabulary: *Match each word with its correct definition. Consider how the word is used in the lesson. This might help you define each term. Use a dictionary to help if necessary.*

a. tragic   d. loot
b. resentment   e. cholera
c. cede

6._____ to carry off or take away; steal

7._____ something disastrous; extremely mournful

8._____ a disease characterized by diarrhea, vomiting, and cramps

9._____ a feeling of displeasure towards another

10._____ to turn over or formally surrender

Guided Reading: *Fill in the blanks below to create complete sentences.*

1. Jealousy of the Cherokee only increased when it was discovered that there might be
_____ on Cherokee lands.

2. *The Cherokee Nation v. Georgia* was thrown out by the high court, but
_____ was decided in favor of the Cherokee.

3. In 1835, the Treaty of New Echota was signed by several Cherokee leaders including
Major Ridge, John Ridge, and _____.

4. Families sitting down to dinner were interrupted by _____
with rifles and bayonets.

5. The Trail of Tears runs more than 2,200 miles and passes through
_____ different states.

History Word Builder: *Match each historical term with its correct definition.*

a. *Cherokee Nation v. Georgia*   d. General Winfield Scott
b. Treaty of New Echota   e. Trail of Tears
c. Major Ridge

6._____The route taken by Native Americans to travel from their tribal lands to their
new home in Indian Territory.

7._____The treaty signed by several Cherokee leaders which resulted in Cherokee
lands being given to the United States.

8._____A Supreme Court case brought by the Cherokee, which was thrown out.

9._____The U.S. Army general responsible for rounding up the Cherokee during the
removal process.

10._____ One of the Cherokee leaders who signed the Treaty of New Echota.

Summarize: *Answer the following questions in the space provided. Attempt to respond in a complete sentence for each question. Be sure to use correct capitalization and punctuation!*

1. Who was the principal chief of the Cherokee during the Indian Removal process?

2. What happened to Cherokee homes and livestock during the removal process?

3. When was the Treaty of New Echota signed?

4. Where did the Cherokee live prior to the removal process?

5. Why was there a fair amount of resentment between the Cherokee and their white neighbors?

6. How did most of the Cherokee react to the Treaty of New Echota?

Student Response: *Write a paragraph addressing the questions raised below. A thorough response should consist of three to five complete sentences.*

7. Imagine you are traveling along the Trail of Tears as the Cherokee are being moved to Indian Territory. Write a brief narrative describing the sights, sounds, and smells you encounter. Be as descriptive as possible. Use additional paper if necessary.

Osceola and the Second Seminole War

Osceola was one of the most important figures of the Seminole removal process. Who was Osceola? Why do people still remember him today?

In 1832, a small group of Seminole chiefs signed the Treaty of Payne's Landing. According to this treaty, the Seminole would give up all rights to their lands in Florida in exchange for land in Indian Territory. Five of the most important chiefs disagreed with the treaty and opposed the idea of Seminole removal. A young warrior named Osceola was also at the negotiations for this treaty. Osceola was against the idea of Seminole removal as well. According to legend, Osceola drew a dagger and stabbed the treaty in disgust.

As a result of their dissent, a United States Indian agent, Wiley Thompson, declared that the Seminole chiefs no longer held their positions of power. He also forbade the sale of weapons and ammunition to the Seminole. On December 28, 1835, Osceola and his followers ambushed Thompson, killing him and six others. That same day, another group of Seminole surrounded 110 U.S. soldiers. Only three soldiers survived. With these two actions, the Seminole had boldly announced that they would not be removed from Florida peacefully. The Second Seminole War had begun.

No white settler or detachment of soldiers was safe. Osceola had vowed to fight to the last drop of Seminole blood. Any group of soldiers venturing into the Florida Everglades had more than Osceola to deal with. The swamps were full of alligators and other dangerous predators. Mosquitos were also dangerous, as they spread malaria.

General Thomas Jesup was sent to Florida with the mission of capturing Osceola and bringing the Seminole resistance to an end. He deceived Osceola by requesting a meeting to discuss peace negotiations. When Osceola arrived, he was apprehended by soldiers and taken away to prison. Even with their brave leader captured, the Seminole did not give up the fight. Two of Osceola's closest followers, Wildcat and Billy Bowlegs, took up the cause and continued fighting against Seminole removal.

They continued the struggle for many years, and eventually, the United States determined to put an end to their efforts. The U.S. government had spent more than $20 million removing the Seminole from Florida and lost more than 1,500 soldiers in the process. More than 3,000 Seminoles had been removed to Indian Territory. This means that for every two Seminole removed, one soldier had died. Several small bands of Seminole were allowed to remain in the Florida Everglades. Those who were removed took up residence in Indian Territory and proceeded building a new society with the other tribes who had been relocated.

Words to watch for:

dissent   forbade

ambushed   speculated

As for Osceola, he lived the remainder of his short life in prison. He died on January 30, 1838, only three months after he had been captured. The official cause of death is unknown, although many have speculated that he died of malaria.

Osceola's life has been remembered in a number of ways. Many songs have been written about him, and his story has been told in more than one major motion picture. Additionally, Florida State University has adopted him as their official mascot. Of course, he is also still loved and remembered by the descendants of those whose land he fought so courageously to protect.

Multiple Choice: *Select the choice that completes the statement or answers the question.*

1._____ Which of the following is not a known fact?
a. In 1832, a group of Seminole chiefs signed the Treaty of Payne's Landing.
b. Five of the most important chiefs disagreed with the signing of the treaty.
c. Osceola was in attendance and also disagreed with the signing of the treaty.
d. Osceola stabbed the Treaty of Payne's Landing with a dagger.

2._____ Which of the following best summarizes the events which led to the
  Second Seminole War?
a. A U.S. Indian Agent declared multiple policies against the Seminole and was killed in retaliation.
b. Andrew Jackson and U.S. soldiers began making unwanted excursions into Florida.
c. The Seminole declared war against the Creek Nation, renewing an old rivalry between the two.
d. Two rival bands of Seminole attacked each other, precipitating a civil war in the Seminole Nation.

3._____ Which of the following best describes how Osceola was captured?
a. He was deceived into attending peace negotiations and was taken away by soldiers.
b. He was ambushed in a swamp and surrounded by soldiers.
c. He was betrayed by one of his top men who told the army of his location.
d. He surrendered willingly, after being told that his family was being held hostage.

4._____ Which of the following statements is inaccurate?
a. The Seminole quickly surrendered after the capture of Osceola.
b. The United States government spent more than $2 million removing the Seminole.
c. More than 3,000 Seminole were removed to Indian Territory.
d. Small bands of Seminole were allowed to remain in the Florida Everglades.

5._____ Which of the following best summarizes Osceola's life after his capture?
a. Osceola was allowed to join his people in Indian Territory and lived for many years.
b. Osceola died after being shot during an attempt to escape from prison.
c. Osceola died in prison only three months after he had been captured.
d. Osceola was paraded around the country and shown to spectators who wanted to see him.

Vocabulary: *Match each word with its correct definition. Consider how the word is used in the lesson. This might help you define each term. Use a dictionary to help if necessary.*

a. dissent
b. forbade
c. ambush

d. vow
e. speculate

6._____ a solemn promise or pledge; a personal commitment

7._____ to have made a rule against; not allow something

8._____ to consider a possibility without knowing all the facts

9._____ attacking by surprise

10._____ a difference of opinion; disagreement

Guided Reading: *Fill in the blanks below to create complete sentences.*

1. United States Indian agent Wiley Thompson forbade the sale of _____ and ammunition to the Seminole.

2. Osceola had vowed to fight to the last drop of Seminole _____.

3. The swamps were full of _____ and other dangerous predators.

4. Two of Osceola's closest followers, _____ and Billy Bowlegs, took up the cause and continued fighting against Seminole removal.

5. Osceola is still loved and remembered by the descendants of those Seminole whose land he so courageously fought to _____.

Correct the Statement: *Each of the following sentences is false. Circle the incorrect word and write the word or phrase that makes the statement correct in the answer blank provided.*

6. In 1832, a group of Seminole chiefs signed the Treaty of Knots Landing. _____.

7. On December 28, 1835, Osceola and his followers ambushed Wiley Johnson, killing him and six others. _____

8. General Thomas Jesup was sent to Florida with the mission of capturing Osceola and bringing the Choctaw resistance to an end. _____.

9. The U.S. government had spent more than $20 million removing the Seminole from Florida and lost more than 15,000 soldiers in the process. _____.

10. Florida University has adopted Osceola as their official mascot. _____.

Summarize: *Answer the following questions in the space provided. Attempt to respond in a complete sentence for each question. Be sure to use correct capitalization and punctuation!*

1. Who was sent to Florida with the mission of capturing Osceola?

2. What were the terms of the Treaty of Payne's Landing?

3. When did Osceola die?

4. Where did the Seminole live?

5. Why were mosquitos so dangerous?

6. How has Osceola been remembered? (List at least one way)

Student Response: *Write a paragraph addressing the questions raised below. A thorough response should consist of three to five complete sentences.*

7. Imagine you have been presented with the same choice as Osceola. Someone is attempting to force you off of the land where your family has lived for hundreds of years. Would you fight for it as Osceola did? Or would you go peacefully? Explain your answer as thoroughly as possible.

Prior to Indian Removal, the Cherokee, Choctaw, Chickasaw, Creek, and Seminole lived in the southern region of the United States. Utilizing internet resources, draw in and label the routes each of these five tribes used to arrive in Indian Territory (Oklahoma). Suggested search terms could include "Trail of Tears routes" or "Indian Removal Routes".

Use a different color for each tribe's route.

Each of the Five Civilized Tribes governed a different portion of Indian Territory. Utilize internet resources to help you identify and draw in the borders of each tribe's territory. Label each one appropriately. Suggested search terms might include "Indian Territory" or "Indian Territory 1820-1854". Keep in mind, the territories should represent the pre-Civil War boundaries. Also label the following cities and forts related to Indian Removal.

Use a different color to shade in each tribe's territory. Cities or forts should be labeled with a •

| Cherokee Territory | Choctaw-Chickasaw Territory | Creek Territory | Seminole Territory |
| Fort Gibson | Tahlequah | Tishomingo | Fort Towson |

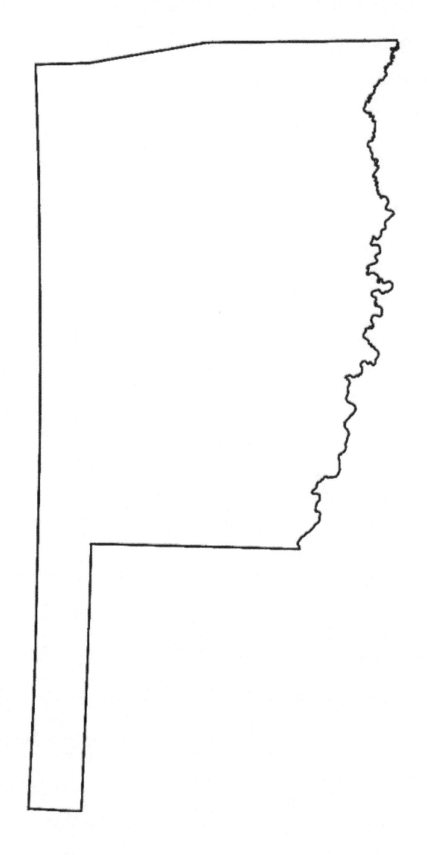

Indian Removal: Post Assessment

Vocabulary: *Match each word with its correct definition.*

a. Trail of Tears
b. Ambush
c. Winfield Scott
d. Cede

e. Fort Gibson
f. Indian Removal Act of 1830
g. Merge
h. Infest

1._____ to turn over or formally surrender

2._____ The route taken by Native Americans to travel from their tribal lands, to their new home in Indian Territory.

3._____ to join together

4._____ overrun with dangerously large numbers

5._____ General who was responsible for moving the Creek west of the Mississippi River.

6._____ The arrival point in Indian Territory for the Creek and many other tribes.

7._____ A law which gave the government official authority to negotiate with Native American tribes for their lands.

8._____ attacking by surprise

Completion: *Fill in the blanks below to create complete sentences.*

| Chickasaw | treaties | Trail of Tears | *Worcester v. Georgia* | Native Americans |
| gold | Elias Boudinot | Osceola | Wildcat | alligators |

9. In the early 1800s, eager white settlers began desiring lands which belonged to

_____.

10. Starting in 1801, a series of _____ had reduced the Choctaw lands to 11,000,000 acres.

11. The _____ paid the Choctaw $530,000 for the westernmost portion of Choctaw land in Indian Territory.

12. Jealousy of the Cherokee only increased when it was discovered that there might be _____ on Cherokee lands.

13. *The Cherokee Nation v. Georgia* was thrown out by the high court, but _____ was decided in favor of the Cherokee.

14. In 1835, the Treaty of New Echota was signed by several Cherokee leaders including Major Ridge, John Ridge, and _____.

15. The _____ runs more than 2,200 miles and passes through nine different states.

16. _____ had vowed to fight to the last drop of Seminole blood.

17. The swamps were full of _____ and other dangerous predators.

18. Two of Osceola's closest followers, _____ and Billy Bowlegs, took up the cause and continued fighting against Seminole removal.

Multiple Choice: *Select the choice that completes the statement or answers the question.*

19._____ Which of the following best explains why land owned by the Five Civilized Tribes was in high demand amongst white settlers?
a. All of their tribal lands were near the coast. This land was highly valuable for overseas trading.
b. All of their tribal lands were near major rivers. These waterways were important for shipping, as well as sources of freshwater.
c. The tribal lands were known to be in spots that would not be severely impacted by natural disasters such as tornadoes and hurricanes.
d. Quality farmland that was rich in minerals was becoming increasingly scarce as more settlers moved into the region.

20._____ Why did the Creek not recognize the Treaty of Indian Springs as legitimate?
a. The treaty had been signed by a different tribe, not the Creek.
b. The treaty had been signed by a chief who did not represent the entire tribe.
c. The treaty had not been signed and dated in the official manner.
d. The treaty had already been nullified by the Supreme Court.

21._____ Which of the following best summarizes what happened to William McIntosh for signing the Treaty of Indian Springs?
a. He was executed by the tribe.
b. He was removed from his position as chief.
c. He was excommunicated from the tribe.
d. He was praised as one of the greatest Creek chiefs in history.

22._____ Which of the following best describes the significance of the Indian Removal Act of 1830?
a. The United States abandoned its efforts to remove Native Americans from their lands and allowed the tribes live in peace.
b. The official policy of the United States became the assimilation of Native Americans into mainstream culture.
c. The official policy of the United States became removing Native Americans from their tribal lands and into Indian Territory.
d. The United States began its effort to locate a piece of land in South America where Native Americans could live in peace.

23._____ Which of the following most accurately describes how the Choctaw who remained in Mississippi were treated?
a. They were treated warmly and encouraged to assimilate into mainstream culture.
b. They were harassed and intimidated in the hopes that they would decide to leave.
c. They were given autonomy and allowed to govern their lands as they saw fit.
d. They were isolated from society and forced to live on reservations.

24._____ Which of the following is *not* one of the reasons why the Chickasaw removal
was less difficult?
a. The Chickasaw removal was controlled by the US government.
b. The Chickasaw were traveling over already established routes.
c. The Chickasaw were allowed to gather and organize their belongings prior to the move.
d. The Chickasaw were moving to a region that had already been settled by the Choctaw.

25._____ Why did the Supreme Court decide that it could not make a ruling in
Cherokee Nation v. Georgia?
a. The Cherokee had not filed the proper paperwork, so their claim was invalid.
b. The state of Georgia had already negotiated a binding contract with the Cherokee.
c. The Supreme Court could only rule on cases involving two different states.
d. The Cherokee Nation was neither an independent nation nor were they citizens of the U.S.

26._____ Which of these most accurately describes the law Georgia passed in an effort to
make life difficult for the Cherokee?
a. Any U.S. citizen living on Cherokee lands had to apply for a license to do so.
b. No citizen of the Cherokee Nation could apply for employment in the state of Georgia.
c. All Cherokee were to report to internment camps and remain there until further notice.
d. The Cherokee were subject to much higher rates of taxation than white citizens.

27._____ Who was Samuel Worcester?
a. He was the highest ranking Chief of the Cherokee Nation.
b. He was the US ambassador who negotiated with the Cherokee.
c. He was a missionary who refused to get a license to live on Cherokee lands.
d. He was a gold prospector who fought to live on Cherokee lands.

28._____ In *Worcester v. Georgia*, the Supreme Court ruled which of the following?
a. The Court ruled that Georgia must return all lands to the Cherokee and pay them
reparations for the wrongs committed.
b. The Court ruled that the state of Georgia was perfectly within its rights to force the
Cherokee from their lands.
c. The Court ruled that Worcester could not have a case heard in court because he
was not a US citizen.
d. The Court ruled that it was the federal government's responsibility to negotiate
with Native American tribes.

29._____ Which president is famously quoted as saying, "John Marshall's made his decision;
now let him enforce it."
a. Abraham Lincoln   c. Andrew Jackson
b. George Washington   d. James Madison

30._____ The Cherokee had lived in which state for hundreds of years?
a. Georgia   c. Kentucky
b. Florida   d. West Virginia

31._____ Which of the following best summarizes Cherokee life during the 1820s?
a. The Cherokee were extremely poor and survived by subsistence farming, eating what they grew.
b. The Cherokee owned plantations, lumber mills, grain mills, and many other successful businesses.
c. The Cherokee lived in huts, wore little clothing, had heavily-tattooed skin, and hunted for food.
d. The Cherokee were coastal fisherman who depended on daily catches to provide food.

32._____ Which of the following best describes the laws that the state of Georgia
        was passing?
a.   The laws were designed to make life miserable for the Cherokee and convince them to leave.
b.   The laws were designed to make life easier for the Cherokee and convince them to stay.
c.   The laws were designed to help the Cherokee preserve their traditional ways of life.
d.   The laws were designed to help the Cherokee assimilate into mainstream culture.

33._____ Which of the following is most significant about the Treaty of New Echota?
a.   The treaty was signed by Major Ridge, John Ridge, and Elias Boudinot.
b.   This was the first removal treaty signed by any of the Five Civilized Tribes.
c.   This was the last of the major removal treaties signed by the Five Civilized Tribes.
d.   The treaty required the Cherokee Nation to cede all of its lands in the Southeast.

34._____ Who was the principal chief of the Cherokee during the removal process?
a.   Sequoyah   c.   Elias Boudinot
b.   Major Ridge   d.   John Ross

35._____ Which of the following best summarizes the Cherokee journey on the Trail of Tears?
a.   Most of the journey was conducted with wagons or on horseback. It was largely a
     smooth transition from Georgia to Indian Territory.
b.   The Cherokee were rounded up and packed into trains. They were then shipped
     hundreds of miles to Indian Territory.
c.   Most of the journey was on foot and during winter. Outbreaks of diseases, lack of
     food, and the harsh conditions resulted in thousands of deaths.
d.   The Cherokee traveled by boat, through the Gulf of Mexico and up the Mississippi
     and Arkansas Rivers to arrive in Indian Territory.

36._____ Which of the following best explains what happened to those who signed the
        Treaty of New Echota?
a.   Those who signed the treaty were viewed as heroes and became the new leaders of the Cherokee.
b.   Those who signed the treaty were viewed as traitors and executed.
c.   Those who signed the treaty had their titles stripped from them and were forced to move
     out of the tribe.
d.   Those who signed the treaty were forced to make a public apology to other tribal members.

37._____ Which of the following best summarizes the events which led to the
        Second Seminole War?
a.   A U.S. Indian Agent declared multiple policies against the Seminole and was killed in retaliation.
b.   Andrew Jackson and U.S. soldiers began making unwanted excursions into Florida.
c.   The Seminole declared war against the Creek Nation, renewing an old rivalry between the two.
d.   Two rival bands of Seminole attacked each other, precipitating a civil war in the Seminole Nation.

38._____ Which of the following made fighting the Seminole in Florida more dangerous?
a.   Soldiers would frequently get trapped in quicksand which was difficult to see.
b.   The soldiers were frequently dehydrated because of the humid conditions.
c.   A mysterious, unknown plague was ravaging the soldiers, leaving many dead.
d.   Mosquitos carried malaria which frequently caused death.

39._____ Which of the following best describes how Osceola was captured?
a. He was deceived into attending peace negotiations and was taken away by soldiers.
b. He was ambushed in a swamp and surrounded by soldiers.
c. He was betrayed by one of his top men who told the army of his location.
d. He surrendered willingly, after being told that his family was being held hostage.

40._____ Which of the following statements is inaccurate?
a. The Seminole quickly surrendered after the capture of Osceola.
b. The United States government spent more than $2 million removing the Seminole.
c. More than 3,000 Seminole were removed to Indian Territory.
d. Small bands of Seminole were allowed to remain in the Florida Everglades.

Major Ridge & Elias Boudinot

Two of the more controversial Cherokee leaders during the removal process were Major Ridge and Elias Boudinot. Who were these men? Why were they so controversial?

Major Ridge was born in present-day Tennessee. He had no formal education and was unable to read or write. However, he was a powerful orator and believed that the Cherokee needed to learn how to communicate with white men.

As a young man, he was initiated as a warrior and fought in the Chickamauga Wars. He also fought for Andrew Jackson at the Battle of Horseshoe Bend during the Creek Wars, as well as during the First Seminole War. During his military service, he earned the rank of Major, a title he eventually adopted and used as his first name throughout the remainder of his life.

As the issue of removal became more prominent, Ridge was initially opposed to the idea, just as most of the Cherokee were. However, he eventually came to the conclusion that the best way to preserve the Cherokee way of life and culture was to move the tribe west of the Mississippi River. He believed the Cherokee should accept the best terms they could receive from the federal government and make the transition peacefully.

On December 29, 1835, he and several others signed the Treaty of New Echota, which ceded all Cherokee lands to the state of Georgia. This treaty was extremely unpopular amongst the Cherokee and those who signed it were vilified. Two years later, in 1837, Ridge moved his family to Indian Territory where they settled at a place called Honey Creek, fifty miles from the other Cherokee settlements.

Elias Boudinot was born in 1802 with the name Gallegina Uwati. The English translation of this name was Buck Watie. His relatives, which included his uncle Major Ridge, were an influential Cherokee family. While attending school, Buck met a man named Elias Boudinot. Boudinot had once been the president of the Second Continental Congress. Boudinot and Watie became acquaintances and Watie asked permission to use his name, and Boudinot agreed. Therefore, Buck Watie became Elias Boudinot.

In 1828, Boudinot was selected as the first editor of the Cherokee newspaper, *The Cherokee Phoenix*. This newspaper was published in both English and the Cherokee language as well (using the Cherokee syllabary developed by Sequoyah just a few years before).

> *Words to watch for:*
>
> *initiated   conclusion*
>
> *vilified   acquaintances*

In the early 1830s, Boudinot became aware that President Andrew Jackson was a supporter of Indian Removal. The Indian Removal Act of 1830, which made removal the official policy of the U.S. government, made it painfully clear to Boudinot that removal was inevitable. He began advocating that the Cherokee accept the best terms possible from the government before they were moved against their will. He used his position as the editor of the newspaper to spread his viewpoint, an opinion that was very unpopular amongst the Cherokee. He was eventually forced to resign as the editor of the *Cherokee Phoenix*.

In 1835, he became one of the tribal leaders who signed the Treaty of New Echota, along with Major Ridge. Not long after, he migrated to Indian Territory to escape hostility from other tribe members.

Eventually, the Cherokee were forcibly removed from Georgia. Following their arrival in Indian Territory, they took retribution on those who had signed the Treaty of New Echota. On June 22, 1839, Elias Boudinot, Major Ridge, and his son John Ridge were all murdered for signing the treaty. Boudinot's brother, Stand Watie, had also signed the treaty. He was attacked this same day, but managed to survive.

Multiple Choice: *Select the choice that completes the statement or answers the question.*

1._____ Which of the following did Major Ridge *not* do?
a.   He fought in the Chickamauga Wars.
b.   He fought with Andrew Jackson at the Battle of Horseshoe Bend.
c.   He fought with Andrew Jackson at the Battle of New Orleans.
d.   He fought with Andrew Jackson during the First Seminole War.

2._____ Why did Major Ridge support the idea of the Cherokee moving west of the Mississippi River?
a.   He had traveled to Indian Territory and truly believed it was better land.
b.   He felt it was the best way to preserve the Cherokee way of life and culture.
c.   He would personally receive a large sum of money from the government.
d.   He believed that there was gold in Indian Territory which he hoped to find.

3._____ Which of the following best summarizes how Buck Watie changed his name to
      Elias Boudinot?
a.   He changed his name after signing the Treaty of New Echota, hoping no one would
      associate him with the treaty.
b.   He found the name in a history book and thought it sounded prestigious.
c.   He was given the name by tribal leaders who believed it would give him good luck.
d.   He took the name from a man he met and admired while attending school.

4._____ Which of the following occupations did Elias Boudinot have?
a.   He was principal chief of the Cherokee.
b.   He was a missionary who worked closely with the Cherokee.
c.   He was the Cherokee representative to the U.S. Congress.
d.   He was the editor of the *Cherokee Phoenix*.

5._____ Which of the following best summarizes what happened to those who signed the
      Treaty of New Echota?
a.   They were executed by the Cherokee who arrived in Indian Territory after the forced removal.
b.   They were treated as heroes and elevated to positions of leadership within the tribe.
c.   They were cast out of the community and essentially kicked out of the tribe.
d.   They were placed in prison for several years for signing the treaty.

Vocabulary: *Match each word with its correct definition. Consider how the word is used in the lesson. This might help you define each term. Use a dictionary to help if necessary.*

a.   orator
b.   initiate
c.   conclusion
d.   vilify
e.   acquaintance

6._____ to admit into a group through a formal ceremony

7._____ a person who is known to another, but not usually a close friend

8._____ a public speaker

9._____ to speak ill of; degrade

10._____ a reasoned deduction; something that has been determined

Guided Reading: *Fill in the blanks below to create complete sentences.*

1. Major Ridge was born in present-day _____.

2. Ridge believed that the Cherokee needed to learn how to
_____ with white men.

3. Ridge believed the Cherokee should accept the best terms it could receive
from the federal _____.

4. The Treaty of _____ was extremely
unpopular amongst the Cherokee and those who signed it were vilified.

5. The English translation of Elias Boudinot's given name was
_____.

6. The *Cherokee Phoenix* was published in both English and the
_____ language.

7. The _____of 1830 made
removal the official policy of the U.S. government.

8. Elias Boudinot was eventually forced to _____ as the
editor of the *Cherokee Phoenix*.

9. Boudinot migrated to Indian Territory to escape _____
from other tribe members.

10. Following their arrival in Indian Territory, the Cherokee took
_____ on those who had signed the Treaty of New Echota.

Summarize: *Answer the following questions in the space provided. Attempt to respond in a complete sentence for each question. Be sure to use correct capitalization and punctuation!*

1. Who signed the Treaty of New Echota, but managed to survive?

2. What happened to most of those who signed the Treaty of New Echota?

3. When was the Treaty of New Echota signed?

4. Where did Major Ridge settle after moving to Indian Territory?

5. Why did Elias Boudinot favor removal?

6. How did Elias Boudinot spread his viewpoint about removal?

Student Response: *Write a paragraph addressing the questions raised below. A thorough response should consist of three to five complete sentences.*

7. Do you feel that those who signed the Treaty of New Echota were given too harsh of a punishment? Or was it justified? Explain your answer.

Sequoyah

One of the most well-known Cherokee was Sequoyah. Who was Sequoyah? Why do so many people remember him today?

Sequoyah was also known by the name George Guess (sometimes spelled Gist), a last name which he shared with his father. Little is known about young Sequoyah, including his date of birth! It is believed he was born between 1770 and 1776. His mother owned a trading post, and Sequoyah spent much of his youth tending cattle, working in the garden, or assisting his mother.

While still a boy, Sequoyah suffered a life-altering injury to his leg. As a result, he walked with the assistance of a crutch most of his life. This injury left him unable to succeed as a farmer or a warrior. Despite this injury, he still served with the Cherokee regiment at the Battle of Horseshoe Bend during the War of 1812.

As he grew older, he became a silversmith and blacksmith. He was self-taught and even constructed his own forge and bellows. Iron items made by Sequoyah were quite popular because he would decorate the items with bits of silver.

Sequoyah had always been impressed by white men's written communications with each other, which he referred to as "talking leaves". Many of the Cherokee believed that writing was a form of witchcraft, but Sequoyah believed that he could create a method for Cherokee to talk to each other on paper, just as the white men did. In about 1809, he began devising a written system of the Cherokee language.

He spent more than a year working on his writing system and experienced many setbacks along the way. At one point, his wife burned all of his notes out of fear that her husband was involved in some form of sorcery. Finally, he developed the Cherokee alphabet, or syllabary. It was a system of 86 characters, one for each syllable in the Cherokee language.

Sequoyah taught his daughter and several others to use the syllabary. After much convincing, the Cherokee Nation finally adopted it as its official alphabet in 1825. Eventually, there was even a newspaper, the *Cherokee Phoenix*, which published in Cherokee and English.

In 1829, Sequoyah moved to a spot near present-day Sallisaw, Oklahoma. He was amongst one of the earliest groups of Cherokee to move from Georgia to their new home in Indian Territory during the removal process. For the remainder of his life, Sequoyah worked diligently to try and resolve the rift that had been created between the Cherokee over the issue of removal.

In 1843, Sequoyah took a trip to Mexico, attempting to locate a band of Cherokee who had migrated there during the removal process. Sometime during this trip, Sequoyah died and was buried somewhere near the border between Mexico and Texas.

> *Words to watch for:*
>
> *blacksmith bellows*
>
> *syllabary diligently*

Sequoyah is remembered in many ways today. A statue of him resides in the National Statuary Hall inside the U.S. Capitol Building. He was the first Native American to be given this honor. In 1980, he was featured on a U.S. postage stamp, he has had no less than eleven schools named in his honor, and his home in Indian Territory has been designated a National Historic Landmark. Also, each year, the state of Oklahoma awards the Sequoyah Award. This is an award voted on by the students of the state, which recognizes the 'best book of the year.'

Multiple Choice: *Select the choice that completes the statement or answers the question.*

1._____ Which of the following best explains why Sequoyah was unable to succeed as a farmer
or warrior?
a. His father left him no land to farm, and he was often criticized as being a coward.
b. His eyesight failed him at a young age, leaving him little ability to perform either occupation.
c. Georgia state law prevented the Cherokee from farming or enlisting in military service.
d. At a young age, his leg was severely injured, leaving him to walk with a crutch most of his life.

2._____ Which of the following statements is false?
a. Sequoyah taught himself how to be a blacksmith.
b. Sequoyah taught himself how to be a silversmith.
c. Sequoyah included bits of gold in the objects he made.
d. Sequoyah constructed his own forge and bellows.

3._____ Which of the following best describes what Sequoyah began attempting to do in about 1809?
a. Sequoyah began attempting to create a new type of metal by blending existing metals.
b. Sequoyah began devising a written system for the Cherokee language.
c. Sequoyah began to negotiate with the U.S. government, trying to save Cherokee tribal lands.
d. Sequoyah began construction of a flying machine, but did not complete the work before he died.

4._____ After his arrival in Indian Territory, Sequoyah spent the remainder of his life doing which of
the following?
a. He tried to resolve the rift created between the Cherokee.
b. He tried to convince the Cherokee to adopt his syllabary.
c. He tried to teach children how adapt to the ways of the white man.
d. He tried to re-establish the Cherokee Nation and make it great again.

5._____ Sequoyah is honored today with all of the following, except?
a. A statue of him resides in National Statuary Hall.
b. In 1980, he was named by *Time Magazine* as one of the 100 Greatest Americans.
c. He has no less than eleven schools named in his honor.
d. The award for children's book of the year in Oklahoma is known as the Sequoyah Award.

Vocabulary: *Match each word with its correct definition. Consider how the word is used in the lesson.
This might help you define each term. Use a dictionary to help if necessary.*

a. blacksmith   d. syllabary
b. forge   e. diligent
c. bellows

6._____ a device used for producing a strong current of air

7._____ a person who makes objects out of iron

8._____ carried out with care and determination

9._____ a special fireplace in which metal is heated for shaping

10._____ a set of written symbols for a given language

Guided Reading: *Fill in the blanks below to create complete sentences.*

1. Sequoyah was also known by the name _____.

2. Despite his injury, Sequoyah still served with the Cherokee regiment at the Battle of Horseshoe Bend during the _____.

3. Iron items made by Sequoyah were quite _____, because he would decorate the items with bits of silver.

4. Sequoyah had always been impressed with white men's _____ communications with each other.

5. Many of the Cherokee believed that writing was a form of _____.

6. The syllabary that Sequoyah created for the Cherokee was a system of _____, one for each syllable in the Cherokee language.

7. The Cherokee Nation adopted Sequoyah's syllabary as its official _____ in 1825.

8. Eventually, there was even a newspaper, the _____, which published in Cherokee and English.

9. Sequoyah was amongst one of the earliest groups of Cherokee to move from Georgia to their new home in _____.

10. In 1843, Sequoyah took a trip to Mexico, attempting to locate a band of Cherokee who had _____ there during the removal process.

Summarize: *Answer the following questions in the space provided. Attempt to respond in a complete sentence for each question. Be sure to use correct capitalization and punctuation!*

1. Who was the first person Sequoyah taught to use his syllabary?

2. What was the name of the Cherokee newspaper?

3. When did the Cherokee Nation adopt Sequoyah's syllabary as its official alphabet?

4. Where was Sequoyah buried?

5. Why is Sequoyah's statue in National Statuary Hall significant?

6. How much time did Sequoyah spend creating his syllabary?

Student Response: *Write a paragraph addressing the questions raised below. A thorough response should consist of three to five complete sentences.*

7. Imagine living in a society with no written language. How different would life be? Name at least three areas of life where a written language is helpful. Explain your answers as thoroughly as possible.

John Ross

One of the most legendary Cherokee leaders was John Ross. Why did John Ross become so notable? How long was he the leader of the Cherokee?

John Ross was born in Turkeytown, in present day Alabama. His given Cherokee name was Guwisguwi. His ethnic heritage included ancestors that were both Cherokee and Scottish. However, he was raised as a full-blood Cherokee. He was exposed to many elements of Cherokee life and participated in different tribal events and ceremonies.

After Ross completed his schooling, he worked for the United States government as an Indian Agent. His skills were useful because he was bilingual, and he could assist in negotiations between the government and the Cherokee. During the War of 1812, he fought for Andrew Jackson at the Battle of Horseshoe Bend. This battle pitted the Cherokee, fighting for the United States, against the Creek, who had allied themselves with the British.

Following the war, John Ross started multiple businesses. He owned a 170 acre tobacco plantation, as well as a ferry crossing. The ferry crossing, known as Ross's Landing, was the foundation for what would eventually become the city of Chattanooga, Tennessee. Through his various business ventures, Ross became quite wealthy. By 1836, he was one of the five wealthiest men in the Cherokee Nation.

In 1824, Ross was one of a small contingent that traveled to Washington D.C. on behalf of the Cherokee. The United States government was attempting to negotiate with the Cherokee in order to purchase their tribal lands. Ross fought this effort and appealed directly to the U.S. Congress. His efforts helped change the relationship between Native American nations and the government. The Cherokee, as well as other tribes, became active defenders of their lands instead of passively negotiating with the government.

In 1827, Ross was selected to help create a new tribal constitution. This constitution called for the election of a principal chief who would serve as the president of the Cherokee Nation. In October 1828, when this new constitution was enacted, John Ross was elected the first principal chief of the Cherokee. He was re-elected to this position many times until his death in 1866.

> **Words to watch for:**
>
> bilingual   contingent
>
> passively   neutral

During the 1830s, the U.S. government was attempting to resettle the Cherokee in Indian Territory. Some of the Cherokee, led by Major Ridge and Elias Boudinot, chose to go peacefully, signing the Treaty of New Echota. John Ross and his followers refused to sign the treaty and resisted removal. This led to the forced removal of the Cherokee to Indian Territory. This event is known as the Trail of Tears. As principal chief, Ross oversaw much of the process and even lost his wife during the removal.

Ross maintained his position of leadership in Indian Territory and helped establish the Cherokee in their new home. During the years of the Civil War, he encouraged his people to stay neutral, but was eventually forced to ally the Cherokee with the Confederacy. Like so many others, Ross lost nearly all of his personal fortune during the war, including his home. One of Ross's sons also died after being captured and sent to prison.

Following the war, Ross once again returned to Washington D.C. to negotiate on behalf of the Cherokee. While in Washington, he became ill and died in 1866, still working to further the Cherokee cause. His body was returned to Park Hill, in Indian Territory, where he was laid to rest. Ross had been the principal chief of the Cherokee for 38 years and had led them through times of great sorrow, as well as great achievements.

Multiple Choice: *Select the choice that completes the statement or answers the question.*

1._____ Which of the following evaluations best explains why John Ross was a
successful Indian Agent?
a. He was well-educated, and since he was bilingual, he could communicate between
the Cherokee and the U.S. government easily.
b. He had many friends who were prominent government officials, which helped
him negotiate favorable terms for the Cherokee.
c. He was ruthless and did not back down when the government made demands.
d. He was a great compromiser, and both sides felt comfortable negotiating with
him because they knew he would be fair.

2._____ How did John Ross help to change the relationship between Native
Americans and the U.S. government?
a. He signed the first removal treaty, which signaled the beginning of the Indian
Removal process.
b. He openly challenged the U.S. Army, declaring war between the United States and
Native Americans.
c. He appealed directly to the U.S. Congress and helped Native Americans become
active defenders of their land.
d. He negotiated a deal with the United States, guaranteeing that all tribes would be
compensated for their tribal lands.

3._____ Which of the following was John Ross chosen to do in 1827?
a. Ross was selected to serve as the Superintendent of Indian Affairs.
b. Ross was appointed to the Council of Elders.
c. Ross was appointed to negotiate with the United States government on
behalf of the Cherokee.
d. Ross was selected to help create a new tribal constitution.

4._____ Which of the following best summarizes John Ross's role during the
Indian Removal process?
a. Ross was one of the few Cherokee chiefs who signed the Treaty of New Echota.
b. Ross was the principal chief of the Cherokee and oversaw much of the removal process.
c. Ross had already retired from public life and passively took part in the removal.
d. Ross was just a child during removal and vowed that he would never let anything like
it happen again.

5._____ Which of the following best describes how John Ross was effected by the
Civil War?
a. Ross owned stock in an ammunition factory and prospered greatly during the war.
b. Ross served as a general during the war and was shot during the Battle of Pea Ridge.
c. Ross lost his son and nearly his entire personal fortune during the war.
d. Ross died just before the war began, so he was not impacted by the war at all.

Guided Reading: *Fill in the blanks below to create complete sentences.*

1. John Ross's given Cherokee name was _____.

2. Ross was raised as a full-blood _____.

3. During the War of 1812, Ross fought for Andrew Jackson at the Battle of
_____.

4. The ferry crossing, known as Ross's Landing, was the foundation for what would eventually become the city of _____, Tennessee.

5. By 1836, he was one of the five _____ men in the Cherokee Nation.

6. In 1824, the United States government was attempting to _____
with the Cherokee in order to purchase their tribal lands.

7. Ross fought the removal effort and appealed directly to the
_____.

8. Some of the Cherokee, led by _____ and Elias Boudinot, chose to go peacefully, signing the Treaty of New Echota.

9. During the years of the Civil War, he encouraged his people to stay neutral, but was eventually forced to ally the Cherokee with the _____.

10.   John Ross had been the principal chief of the Cherokee for
_____.

Vocabulary: *Match each word with its correct definition. Consider how the word is used in the lesson. This might help you define each term. Use a dictionary to help if necessary.*

a. bilingual
b. pit
c. contingent

d. passive
e. neutral

11._____ to match in opposition against one another

12._____ not reacting visibly, nor participating actively

13._____ not taking one side or the other in a dispute

14._____ the ability to speak two different languages

15._____ a group representing a larger body of people

Summarize: *Answer the following questions in the space provided. Attempt to respond in a complete sentence for each question. Be sure to use correct capitalization and punctuation.*

1. Who signed the Treaty of New Echota along with Major Ridge?

2. What position was John Ross elected to in 1828?

3. When did John Ross die?

4. Where did John Ross travel in 1824, on behalf of the Cherokee?

5. Why were the Cherokee fighting against the Creek in the War of 1812?

6. How did John Ross become so wealthy?

Student Response: *Write a paragraph addressing the questions raised below. A thorough response should consist of three to five complete sentences.*

7. John Ross was the principal chief of the Cherokee from 1828 to 1866. Do you feel leaders should be in power for this long? Why or why not? Support your answer as thoroughly as possible.

Stand Watie

Stand Watie became one of the most prominent Native American figures of the Civil War. How did Stand Watie become so important? How is he remembered today?

Stand Watie was born on December 12, 1806 in the Cherokee Nation (in Georgia). His given name was Degataga Uwatie. The name Degataga meant "to stand firm". As he became older, and went to school to learn English, he changed his name to the English translation and became known as Stand Watie.

Watie's brother, Elias Boudinot, and uncle, Major Ridge, were both prominent and outspoken members of the Cherokee tribe. While Stand was quieter than his relatives, he always stood by them and supported their decisions. In 1835, all three men were amongst those who signed the Treaty of New Echota. This treaty was signed by those who felt the Cherokee should move peacefully to Indian Territory rather than being forced off their Georgia lands. The treaty was highly unpopular amongst the Cherokee and eventually cost Major Ridge and Elias Boudinot their lives. Following the deaths of his uncle and brother, Stand Watie became the default leader for those Cherokee who had followed them.

In 1861, at the outbreak of the Civil War, Watie immediately volunteered his services to the Confederacy. A large number of Cherokee joined him, pledging to follow wherever he may lead. He was given the rank of colonel and authorized to form a Native American regiment. This regiment became known as the Cherokee Mounted Rifles. Watie and his men stood out at several battles, including the Battle of Pea Ridge where Watie's forces held their position to the very end and were the last to retreat.

As a commanding officer, Watie was loved by his men. They believed he genuinely cared about them as they saw his kindness in action. He would frequently give up his own meals to make sure soldiers had enough to eat, or sacrifice his blanket to a soldier who didn't have one. He spent large amounts of his own wealth to buy saddles, boots, and uniforms which his men desperately needed.

Watie never order a charge he did not lead personally. Despite this habit of being out in front of his men, he never received a wound throughout the war. This led many of his fellow soldiers to believe that he was invincible and could not be harmed by bullets.

Watie's leadership abilities did not go without notice. He was named principal chief of the Cherokee in 1862, adding to his list of responsibilities. He was also granted the title of brigadier general by Jefferson Davis in 1864. This made him one of only two Native Americans to achieve this rank during the Civil War.

> *Words to watch for:*
>
> *default   retreat*
>
> *sacrifice   invincible*

Watie fought bravely throughout the war, raiding supply lines and performing hit-and-run campaigns on several different forts. The Cherokee Mounted Rifles also fought in a number of battles and skirmishes in Indian Territory, Arkansas, Texas, Kansas, and Missouri. It has been stated that Watie's forces fought in more battles west of the Mississippi River than any other unit. At the war's conclusion, General Stand Watie had the honor of being the last Confederate general to surrender, which he did on June 23, 1865.

Following the war, Watie retired from public life and attempted to rebuild his personal fortune. He died on September 9, 1871 and was buried in Tahlequah, Oklahoma. Watie is remembered by many as a great Cherokee, and a great American. There is a memorial in his honor in Tahlequah, and his Civil War deeds have also been portrayed in the historical fiction novel *Rifles for Watie* by Harold Keith.

©Reading Through History

Multiple Choice: *Select the choice that completes the statement or answers the question.*

1._____ Which of the following correctly identifies the meaning of Degataga Uwatie?
a. "to walk away"   c. "to stand firm"
b. "to lead boldly"   d. "to follow loyally"

2._____ Which of the following best summarizes Stand Watie's actions at the outbreak of the
               Civil War?
a. He volunteered his services to the Confederacy and formed a Native American regiment known as the
    Cherokee Mounted Rifles.
b. He volunteered his services to the Union and was immediately given the rank of brigadier general.
c. He sold all of his property and left the country as quickly as he could. He lived in Mexico throughout
    the war and returned after it was over.
d. He wrote a letter to the leader of both sides, encouraging them to end the violence before it destroyed
    the nation that he loved.

3._____ Which of the following best describes Stand Watie's leadership style?
a. He was often thought of as cold and heartless, giving little care for his men's safety.
b. He was distant from his men, but they respected him because of his success on the battlefield.
c. He was loved by his men, but often criticized for his lack of true leadership abilities.
d. He was very personal, leading from the front and genuinely cared about his men.

4._____ Which of the following statements about Stand Watie is inaccurate?
a. He was named the principal chief of the Cherokee in 1862.
b. He was given the rank of brigadier general in 1864.
c. He was one of many Native Americans to hold the rank of general during the Civil War.
d. He and his forces fought in more battles west of the Mississippi River than any other unit.

5._____ Which of the following best describes Stand Watie's actions at the conclusion of the Civil War?
a. He returned to the United States and made a fortune off of rebuilding destroyed Southern cities.
b. He became the last Confederate general to surrender in June of 1865.
c. He helped negotiate the peace agreement between the Union and the Confederacy.
d. He refused to surrender, continuing to fight the war for several more years after its conclusion.

Vocabulary: *Match each word with its correct definition. Consider how the word is used in the lesson.*
This might help you define each term. Use a dictionary to help if necessary.

a. default   d. invincible
b. retreat   e. skirmish
c. sacrifice

6._____ to surrender or give up, for the sake of something else

7._____ the forced withdrawal of an army during a battle

8._____ a fight between small numbers of troops; a minor battle

9._____ incapable of being conquered or defeated; cannot be harmed

10._____ something that is selected in the absence of a better alternative

Guided Reading: *Fill in the blanks below to create complete sentences.*

1. Stand Watie was born on December 12, 1806 in the
_____.

2. In 1835, all three men were amongst those who signed the Treaty of
_____.

3. The treaty was highly unpopular amongst the Cherokee and eventually cost Major Ridge and Elias Boudinot their _____.

4. At the outbreak of the Civil War, Stand Watie was given the rank of
_____ and authorized to form a Native American regiment.

5. Watie and his men stood out at several battles, including the Battle of
_____.

6. Watie spent large amounts of his own wealth to buy saddles, boots, and
_____.

7. Watie never order a charge he did not lead _____.

8. Watie was granted the title of brigadier general by _____
in 1864.

9. Watie fought bravely throughout the war, raiding supply lines and performing
_____ campaigns on several different forts.

10. Following the war, Watie retired from public life and attempted to rebuild his personal _____.

Summarize: *Answer the following questions in the space provided. Attempt to respond in a complete sentence for each question. Be sure to use correct capitalization and punctuation!*

1. Who was Stand Watie's brother?

2. What was the title of the book written by Harold Keith?

3. When did Stand Watie surrender?

4. Where was Stand Watie buried?

5. Why did Major Ridge and Elias Boudinot lose their lives?

6. How did Stand Watie's men grow to love him? (Why?)

Student Response: *Write a paragraph addressing the questions raised below. A thorough response should consist of three to five complete sentences.*

7. It is difficult for anyone to fight in a war. However, do you feel it would have been easier to fight for someone like Stand Watie? Why or why not? Explain your answer as thoroughly as possible.

There were many prominent Cherokee leaders who lived in the southern region of the United States. Utilize a map of the United States, map of Oklahoma, or internet resources to help you locate and label the following locations mentioned in this unit.

Label battlefields with an X. Cities should be labeled with a •

New Echota   Turkeytown   Horseshoe Bend Battlefield   Tahlequah
Chattanooga   Park Hill   Indian Territory   Georgia

Color each labeled state or territory a different color.

Cherokee Leaders: Post Assessment

Vocabulary: *Match each word with its correct definition.*

a. bilingual   d. syllabary
b. blacksmith   e. neutral
c. retreat   f. skirmish

1._____ not taking one side or the other in a dispute

2._____ the ability to speak two different languages

3._____ a person who makes objects out of iron

4._____ a set of written symbols for a given language

5._____ the forced withdrawal of an army during a battle

6._____ a fight between small numbers of troops; a minor battle

Multiple Choice: *Select the choice that completes the statement or answers the question.*

7._____ Why did Major Ridge support the idea of the Cherokee moving west of the Mississippi River?
a. He had traveled to Indian Territory and truly believed it was better land.
b. He felt it was the best way to preserve the Cherokee way of life and culture.
c. He would personally receive a large sum of money from the government.
d. He believed that there was gold in Indian Territory which he hoped to find.

8._____ Which of the following best summarizes how Buck Watie changed his name to Elias Boudinot?
a. He changed his name after signing the Treaty of New Echota, hoping no one would associate him with the treaty.
b. He found the name in a history book and thought it sounded prestigious.
c. He was given the name by tribal leaders who believed it would give him good luck.
d. He took the name from a man he met and admired while attending school.

9._____ Which of the following occupations did Elias Boudinot have?
a. He was principal chief of the Cherokee.
b. He was a missionary who worked closely with the Cherokee.
c. He was the Cherokee representative to the U.S. Congress.
d. He was the editor of the *Cherokee Phoenix*.

10._____ Which of the following best describes how Elias Boudinot spread his viewpoint about the removal process?
a. Boudinot published his opinions in *The Cherokee Phoenix*.
b. Boudinot was a fiery public speaker and preached his message on street corners.
c. Boudinot tried to appeal directly to the president about the issue of removal.
d. Boudinot spoke to the U.S. Congress regarding the issue of removal.

11._____ Which of the following best summarizes what happened to those who signed the Treaty of New Echota?
a. They were executed by the Cherokee who arrived in Indian Territory after the forced removal.
b. They were treated as heroes and elevated to positions of leadership within the tribe.
c. They were cast out of the community and essentially kicked out of the tribe.
d. They were placed in prison for several years for signing the treaty.

12._____ Which of the following best explains why Sequoyah was unable to succeed as a farmer or warrior?
a. His father left him no land to farm, and he was often criticized as being a coward.
b. His eyesight failed him at a young age, leaving him little ability to perform either occupation.
c. Georgia state law prevented the Cherokee from farming or enlisting in military service.
d. At a young age, his leg was severely injured, leaving him to walk with a crutch most of his life.

13._____ Which of the following best describes what Sequoyah began attempting to do in about 1809?
a. Sequoyah began attempting to create a new type of metal by blending existing metals.
b. Sequoyah began devising a written system for the Cherokee language.
c. Sequoyah began to negotiate with the U.S. government, trying to save Cherokee tribal lands.
d. Sequoyah began construction of a flying machine, but did not complete the work before he died.

14._____ After his arrival in Indian Territory, Sequoyah spent the remainder of his life doing which of the following?
a. He tried to resolve the rift created between the Cherokee.
b. He tried to convince the Cherokee to adopt his syllabary.
c. He tried to teach children how adapt to the ways of the white man.
d. He tried to re-establish the Cherokee Nation and make it great again.

15._____ Which of the following best explains why Sequoyah's statue in National Statuary Hall is significant?
a. His statue was the first statue to be placed in the National Statuary Hall.
b. He was the first Native American to be honored with such a statue.
c. His statue was the last statue to be placed in the National Statuary Hall.
d. He is the only non-politician to ever be honored with such a statue.

16._____ Why did the Cherokee fight against the Creek during the War of 1812?
a. The Creek had allied themselves with the British.
b. The Cherokee had a long-standing feud with the Creek.
c. The Creek were engaged in violent attacks against the Cherokee.
d. The Cherokee did not participate in the War of 1812.

17._____ How did John Ross help to change the relationship between Native Americans and the U.S. government?
a. He signed the first removal treaty, which signaled the beginning of the Indian Removal process.
b. He openly challenged the U.S. Army, declaring war between the United States and Native Americans.
c. He appealed directly to the U.S. Congress and helped Native Americans become active defenders of their land.
d. He negotiated a deal with the United States, guaranteeing that all tribes would be compensated for their tribal lands.

18._____ Which of the following was John Ross chosen to do in 1827?
a. Ross was selected to serve as the Superintendent of Indian Affairs.
b. Ross was appointed to the Council of Elders.
c. Ross was appointed to negotiate with the United States government on behalf of the Cherokee.
d. Ross was selected to help create a new tribal constitution.

19._____ Which of the following best summarizes John Ross's role during the Indian Removal process?
a. Ross was one of the few Cherokee chiefs who signed the Treaty of New Echota.
b. Ross was the principal chief of the Cherokee and oversaw much of the removal process.
c. Ross had already retired from public life and passively took part in the removal.
d. Ross was just a child during removal and vowed that he would never let anything like it happen again.

20._____ Which of the following best describes how John Ross was effected by the Civil War?
a. Ross owned stock in an ammunition factory and prospered greatly during the war.
b. Ross served as a general during the war and was shot during the Battle of Pea Ridge.
c. Ross lost his son and nearly his entire personal fortune during the war.
d. Ross died just before the war began, so he was not impacted by the war at all.

21._____ Which of the following correctly identifies the meaning of Degataga Uwatie?
a. "to walk away"   c. "to stand firm"
b. "to lead boldly"   d. "to follow loyally"

22._____ Which of the following people signed the Treaty of New Echota but avoided execution?
a. John Ross   c. Elias Boudinot
b. Major Ridge   d. Stand Watie

23._____ Which of the following individuals was Stand Watie's brother?
a. John Ross   c. Elias Boudinot
b. Sequoyah   d. Major Ridge

24._____ Which of the following best summarizes Stand Watie's actions at the outbreak of the Civil War?
a. He volunteered his services to the Confederacy and formed a Native American regiment known as the Cherokee Mounted Rifles.
b. He volunteered his services to the Union and was immediately given the rank of brigadier general.
c. He sold all of his property and left the country as quickly as he could. He lived in Mexico throughout the war and returned after it was over.
d. He wrote a letter to the leader of both sides, encouraging them to end the violence before it destroyed the nation that he loved.

25._____ Which of the following best describes Stand Watie's leadership style?
a. He was often thought of as cold and heartless, giving little care for his men's safety.
b. He was distant from his men, but they respected him because of his success on the battlefield.
c. He was loved by his men, but often criticized for his lack of true leadership abilities.
d. He was very personal, leading from the front and genuinely cared about his men.

26._____ Which of the following best describes Stand Watie's actions at the conclusion of the
                Civil War?
a.   He returned to the United States and made a fortune off of rebuilding destroyed Southern cities.
b.   He became the last Confederate general to surrender in June of 1865.
c.   He helped negotiate the peace agreement between the Union and the Confederacy.
d.   He refused to surrender, continuing to fight the war for several more years after its conclusion.

Completion: *Fill in the blanks below to create complete sentences.*

Witchcraft	86 characters	New Echota	Cherokee
Indian Territory	War of 1812	George Guess	

27. The Treaty of _____ was extremely unpopular amongst the
Cherokee and those who signed it were vilified.

28. The *Cherokee Phoenix* was published in both English and the _____
language.

29. Sequoyah was also known by the name _____.

30. Despite his injury, Sequoyah still served with the Cherokee regiment at the Battle of Horseshoe
Bend during the _____.

31. Many of the Cherokee believed that writing was a form of _____.

32. The syllabary that Sequoyah created for the Cherokee was a system of
_____, one for each syllable in the Cherokee language.

33. Sequoyah was amongst one of the earliest groups of Cherokee to move from Georgia to their new
home in _____.

Completion: *Fill in the blanks below to create complete sentences.*

Chattanooga	Pea Ridge	Confederacy	wealthiest
Horseshoe Bend	Principal Chief	Brigadier General	

34. During the War of 1812, Ross fought for Andrew Jackson at the Battle of
_____.

35. The ferry crossing known as Ross's Landing was the foundation for what would eventually
become the city of _____, Tennessee.

36. By 1836, John Ross was one of the five _____ men in the Cherokee Nation.

37. During the years of the Civil War, John Ross encouraged his people to stay neutral, but was
eventually forced to ally the Cherokee with the _____.

38. John Ross was the _____ of the Cherokee for 38 years.

39. Stand Watie and his men stood out at several battles, including the Battle of
_____.

40. Stand Watie was granted the title of _____ by Jefferson
Davis in 1864.

The Civil War in Indian Territory

The Civil War affected the entire nation, including Indian Territory. Which side did Indian Territory join during the war? Were there any battles fought there?

At the outbreak of the Civil War, the tribal nations living in Indian Territory had a tough decision to make. Some felt that they should support the Union and help preserve the United States of America. Others felt that it was natural for them to join the Confederate States of America. All of the tribes had originally come from Southern states such as Georgia, Alabama, and Tennessee. They shared a similar culture and way of life with the Southerners. Many still had relatives living in those Southern states.

Additionally, the Confederacy was making a strong effort to recruit Indian Territory to its cause. The Confederacy saw much value in the territory. There were herds of cattle that could be used for beef and leather. The territory also had horses for the cavalry, farms that could provide grain, large deposits of lead for ammunition, and plentiful supplies of salt as well. Also, Confederate leaders hoped to use Indian Territory as a buffer zone between Texas and Kansas. In February of 1861, the Confederacy sent a representative to Indian Territory. By May, four of the five tribes had allied themselves with the Confederacy. Only the Cherokee remained neutral.

Confederate Troops moved in from Texas and quickly occupied Fort Washita, Fort Arbuckle, Fort Gibson, and Fort Cobb. In August of 1861, Confederate General Sterling Price won a solid victory in Missouri at the Battle of Wilson's Creek. This victory convinced the Cherokee to side with the Confederacy as well.

> *Words to watch for:*
>
> *cavalry   neutral*
>
> *decisive   guerilla*

Opothleyahola

Many Native Americans did not want to become involved in the war at all. They saw this as a choice between supporting the states that forced them to move off of their tribal lands or supporting the federal government that allowed them to do it. A Creek leader named Opothleyahola established a neutral camp at the Deep Fork River and encouraged all those who wished to stay neutral to join him. Over 7,000 Native Americans joined him, mostly fellow Creeks and Seminoles. Unfortunately, Confederate leaders were suspicious of such a large group of neutrals living in Confederate territory.

Fearing that they would eventually side with the Union, the Confederacy sent General Douglas Cooper to hunt down Opothleyahola's followers. He and his soldiers attacked at a place called Round Mountain and again at Bird Creek. After a third engagement, Opothleyahola and his followers fled Indian Territory into Kansas. Many joined the Union Army, but others were still determined to stay neutral.

As the war progressed, there were a few significant engagements in or close to Indian Territory. The Battle of Pea Ridge occurred in Arkansas, in March of 1862. Over 800 Cherokee troops led by General Stand Watie participated in the battle. They were a part of more than 16,000 Confederates who fought that day. The Union prevailed at Pea Ridge, with more than 4,600 Confederates losing their lives.

The Battle of Cabin Creek proved important as well. At this battle, the First Kansas Colored Infantry saw significant action. These were African American soldiers fighting for the Union. They and their fellow Union soldiers protected a Union supply train as it made its way to Fort Gibson, which the Union had recently recaptured. This marked the first time during the Civil War that Native American soldiers, African American soldiers, and white soldiers had fought alongside each other.

The most significant battle to take place in Indian Territory was the Battle of Honey Springs, which occurred on August 26th, 1863. Under the command of General James G. Blunt, Union troops won a resounding victory that became decisive in the battle for control over Indian Territory. Shortly after this, Fort Smith was captured by Union forces. The capture of Fort Smith meant that Indian Territory was cut off from the Arkansas River, and Confederate forces would receive very little aid for the remainder of the war.

The final two years of the war in Indian Territory saw a significant amount of guerilla combat. These were hit-and-run campaigns in which targets would be struck and then the forces would retreat quickly. These types of raids were often conducted to acquire food, weapons, or other needed supplies.

The most successful of these guerilla raiders was Colonel William Quantrill and his Confederate horsemen known as Quantrill's Raiders. Quantrill mostly operated in Missouri and Kansas, but was known to hit targets in Indian Territory as well. General Stand Watie and his men also conducted similar types of guerilla raids throughout Indian Territory.

The Civil War finally came to an end on April 9, 1865. Indian Territory, a reluctant participant in the conflict, had been devastated by the war. Thousands were dead, livestock had been raided and slaughtered, and homes and fields had been destroyed. With the war behind them, the people of the territory, just like the rest of the South, began the long process of rebuilding.

William Quantrill

Multiple Choice: *Select the choice that completes the statement or answers the question.*

1._____ Which of the following was *not* amongst the reasons that many in the tribal nations wanted to join the Confederacy?
a. All of the tribes had originally come from Southern states.
b. They shared a similar culture and way of life to those living in Southern states.
c. They felt it was necessary in order to preserve the United States of America.
d. Many still had relatives living in Southern states.

2._____ Which of the following was *not* one of the reasons the Confederacy hoped to persuade Indian Territory into joining them?
a. There were herds of cattle that could be used for beef and leather.
b. There were large deposits of lead which could be used for ammunition.
c. The Confederacy hoped to use Indian Territory as a base to set up trade with Mexico.
d. It was hoped that Indian Territory could serve as a buffer zone between Kansas and Texas.

3._____ Which of the following best explains why many Native Americans did not want to become involved in the war at all?
a. They saw it as a choice between those who had forced them off of their tribal land and the federal government that had allowed them to do it.
b. As a general rule, the Native American tribes had always been very peaceful and avoided violence at all costs.
c. Most of the tribes realized that regardless of which side they joined, there would be major retribution from the other.
d. Most believed that since they were independent nations, they should declare their neutrality and wait to sign a trade agreement with the victorious side.

4._____ Which of the following best explains the significance of the Battle of Honey Springs?
a. General James G. Blunt won a resounding victory, allowing him to move on to greater fame.
b. This was the only battle that was actually fought in Indian Territory throughout the entire war.
c. Fort Smith was captured by Union forces, cutting Indian Territory off from the Arkansas River.
d. It was the first battle in which Native American soldiers played a major role in the fighting.

5._____ Which of the following best describes the type of fighting that Quantrill's Raiders became well-known for?
a. They were fierce fighters who were well-known for always being on the frontlines of every battle.
b. They were a network of spies that kept their eye on Union troop movements.
c. They were a cavalry unit that frequently supported infantry troops during engagements.
d. They conducted guerilla raids in which they struck targets quickly before disappearing.

Vocabulary: *Match each word with its correct definition. Consider how the word is used in the lesson. This might help you define each term. Use a dictionary to help if necessary.*

a. cavalry
b. buffer
c. neutral

d. decisive
e. guerilla

1._____ a military force composed of troops on horseback

2._____ crucial or important

3._____ a shield to protect against harm or to reduce dangerous interaction

4._____ not taking part in a dispute

5._____ a small armed force that is usually dependent on hit-and-run tactics

Guided Reading: *Fill in the blanks below to create complete sentences.*

6. The Confederacy was making a strong effort to _____ Indian Territory to its cause.

7. By May of 1861, four of the five tribes had allied themselves with the _____.

8. Confederate Troops moved in from Texas and quickly occupied Fort _____, Fort Arbuckle, Fort Gibson and Fort Cobb.

9. Confederate leaders were _____ of such a large group of neutrals living in Confederate territory.

10. General Douglas Cooper and his Confederate soldiers attacked neutral Indians at a place called

_____.

Correct the Statement: *Each of the following sentences is false. Circle the incorrect word and write the word or phrase that makes the statement correct in the answer blank provided.*

11. The Battle of Pea Ridge occurred in southern Kansas, in March of 1862.

_____.

12. At the Battle of Cabin Creek, the First Arkansas Colored Infantry saw significant action.

_____.

13. With Fort Smith in Confederate hands, that meant that Indian Territory would receive little aid for the remainder of the war. _____.

14. Guerilla raids were often conducted to acquire warships, weapons, or other needed supplies.

_____.

15. The Civil War came to an end on April 9, 1781. _____.

Summarize: *Answer the following questions in the space provided. Attempt to respond in a complete sentence for each question. Be sure to use correct capitalization and punctuation!*

1. Who was the Creek leader that established a neutral camp at the Deep Fork River?

2. What convinced the Cherokee to side with the Confederacy?

3. When was the Battle of Honey Springs?

4. Where did Quantrill's Raiders conduct most of their raids?

5. Why was the Battle of Cabin Creek said to be significant?

6. How well off was Indian Territory following the Civil War? (What condition was it in?)

Student Response: *Write a paragraph addressing the questions raised below. A thorough response should consist of three to five complete sentences.*

7. Based on the information provided in the lesson, do you feel that the tribal nations made the correct decision in joining the Confederacy? Should they have sided with the Union? Should they have stayed neutral? If applicable, cite specific textual evidence to support your answer. Explain your answer as thoroughly as possible.

There were many prominent sites in Indian Territory during the Civil War. Utilize a map of Oklahoma or internet resources to help you locate and label the following locations.

Rivers should be drawn in blue and labeled. Battlefields should be labeled with an X. Forts should be labeled with a ☐

Battle of Round Mountain (near Yale, OK)
Battle of Honey Springs (Near Checotah, OK)
Fort Washita
Fort Gibson

Battle of Cabin Creek (near Cabin Creek, OK)
Arkansas River
Fort Arbuckle
Fort Cobb

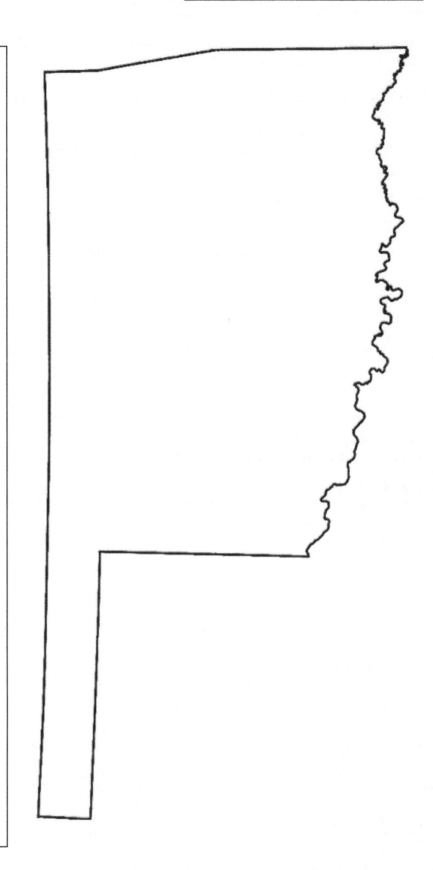

Geronimo

Geronimo became one of the most feared names in the Old West. Who was Geronimo? What did he do to become so well-known?

In the years after the Civil War, the United States began to settle regions in the western portion of the nation. The territory that would become Arizona and New Mexico had been acquired from Mexico during the Mexican War, but the nation had been distracted by the Civil War and never settled the area.

There were many Native American tribes already living in this region, and the United States government began efforts to resettle them in Indian Territory, just as had been done with the Five Civilized Tribes in the 1830s. These western tribes included the Kiowa, Comanche, Cheyenne, Arapaho, and Apache. The Apache occupied a portion of southwestern Arizona and had been struggling against white settlers since the days of the first Spanish explorers in the 1500s.

In 1861, an Apache leader named Cochise was accused of kidnapping a rancher's son. He was tracked down and captured by the U.S. Army. Cochise managed to escape, but in response to his escape, the Army hanged three of Cochise's relatives. From that point forward, Cochise and his followers began a war against white settlers. Cochise eventually died of stomach cancer, but others would carry on his cause. One of those was a young Apache medicine man named Goyathlay.

In 1858, when Goyathlay was about 30 years old, he returned from a trip to Mexico and discovered that his village had been attacked by Mexican troops. Amongst the dead were his mother, his young wife, and his three children. Goyathlay's ensuing rampage would make him the most feared Apache medicine man ever.

Words to watch for:
impervious   elusive
apprehend   inaugural

His battle skills were unmatched and both Mexican and American settlers were terrified of him. Some attributed supernatural powers to him. They claimed he could see into the future, walk across sand without leaving footprints, and that he was even impervious to bullets. The Mexicans had such respect for this warrior that they nicknamed him Geronimo. It is this name that most remember Goyathlay by today.

Geronimo and his band of followers terrorized the southwest throughout the 1870s and 1880s, resisting all efforts by the U.S. Army to remove them from their lands. Regardless of the Army's efforts, they seemed unable to capture the elusive medicine man. At one point, there were more than 5,000 troops searching for and attempting to apprehend Geronimo and his band of less than 50 followers. In September of 1886, Geronimo surrendered for the final time. He was given a prison sentence and taken across the country. He was eventually allowed to settle with his people in Indian Territory. He lived out the rest of his life at Fort Sill in present-day Oklahoma.

In his later years, he made public appearances, posed for pictures, sold his autograph for 50 cents apiece, and performed in Wild West Shows, including the famous 101 Ranch Wild West Show. He even participated in Theodore Roosevelt's inaugural parade in 1905.

Geronimo died at the age of 80, after suffering from pneumonia. However, his legacy still lives on today. Many books have been written about his life, and there have been multiple efforts to convey his story in motion pictures.

Multiple Choice: *Select the choice that completes the statement or answers the question.*

1._____ Which of the following best explains why the nation had never settled the regions of New Mexico and Arizona?
a.   The region was a desert and no one wanted to settle there.
b.   The Apache were so fierce that no one dared to settle in the area.
c.   The president had outlawed any settlement until the year 1870.
d.   The nation had become distracted by the Civil War.

2._____ Which of the following best summarizes why Cochise started a war against white settlers?
a.   The U.S. Army had hanged three of his relatives.
b.   Cochise had been kidnapped as a boy and forced to be a slave for a white family.
c.   Cochise was an Apache chief who had been tricked into signing a removal treaty.
d.   The president had personally insulted Cochise's tribe.

3._____ Which of the following abilities was *not* attributed to Geronimo?
a.   Some believed he could see into the future.
b.   Others thought he could walk across sand without leaving footprints.
c.   Some believed he could turn himself into an animal in order to escape.
d.   Others believed that he was impervious to bullets.

4._____ Which of the following best summarizes the efforts to capture Geronimo?
a.   Geronimo was tricked into attending a peace conference. When he arrived he was apprehended without a struggle.
b.   More than 5,000 soldiers attempted to capture Geronimo and his followers throughout the 1870s and '80s.
c.   The pursuit of Geronimo continued for years until the hunt was finally discontinued. Geronimo was allowed to live out his life in Arizona.
d.   Geronimo briefly evaded capture, but knew his cause was hopeless. He quickly surrendered and retired to life in Indian Territory.

5._____ Which of the following accurately describes Geronimo's final years?
a.   He lived at Fort Sill in Indian Territory and performed in Wild West shows.
b.   He disappeared into the mountains of Mexico, never to be seen again.
c.   He was shot and killed by U.S. soldiers in one last, final standoff.
d.   He was taken to a prison in Washington D.C. where he lived out his life.

Vocabulary: *Match each word with its correct definition. Consider how the word is used in the lesson. This might help you define each term. Use a dictionary to help if necessary.*

a.   supernatural   d.   apprehend
b.   impervious   e.   inaugural
c.   elusive

6._____ beyond what is natural; unexplainable by natural law

7._____ difficult to catch

8._____ something which marks the beginning

9._____ incapable of being injured; cannot be penetrated

10._____ to take custody of; catch

Guided Reading: *Fill in the blanks below to create complete sentences.*

1. In the years after the Civil War, the United States began to settle regions in the _____ portion of the nation.

2. Amongst the western tribes that were removed were the Kiowa, Comanche, Cheyenne, Arapaho, and _____.

3. In 1861, an Apache leader, _____, was accused of kidnapping a rancher's son.

4. Geronimo's battle skills were unmatched and both Mexican and American settlers were _____ of him.

5. In his later years, Geronimo made public appearances, posed for pictures, and sold his autograph for _____ apiece.

Correct the Statement: *Each of the following sentences is false. Circle the incorrect word(s) and write the word or phrase that makes the statement correct in the answer blank provided.*

6. The territory that would become Arizona and New Mexico had been acquired from Mexico during the Spanish-American War. _____.

7. The Apache occupied a portion of southwestern Arizona and had been struggling against white settlers since the days of the French explorers in the 1500s. _____.

8. The Native Americans had such respect for Goyathlay that they nicknamed him Geronimo. _____.

9. Geronimo and his band of followers terrorized the northwest throughout the 1870s and 1880s. _____.

10. Geronimo performed in Wild West shows, including the famous Pawnee Bill's Wild West Show. _____.

Summarize: *Answer the following questions in the space provided. Attempt to respond in a complete sentence for each question. Be sure to use correct capitalization and punctuation!*

1. Whose inaugural parade did Geronimo appear in?

2. What was Geronimo's real name?

3. When did Geronimo surrender for the final time?

4. Where did Geronimo live out his remaining days?

5. Why did Geronimo begin his war against Mexicans and white settlers?

6. How did Geronimo die?

Student Response: *Write a paragraph addressing the questions raised below. A thorough response should consist of three to five complete sentences.*

7. Why do you suppose Geronimo was taken to a prison far across the country when he was first arrested?

Black Kettle

Black Kettle is a widely remembered Cheyenne chief. What did Black Kettle do? Where did he live?

The Cheyenne and Arapaho tribes had always kept the peace with white settlers who moved into Colorado. Even when gold was discovered at Pike's Peak in 1858, and settlers poured in from all over the country, the two tribes remained peaceful. As more and more settlers continued to arrive, the Cheyenne and Arapaho had to continue moving further and further west to do their hunting.

Even though the Cheyenne were largely peaceful, many of the settlers felt nervous about their presence. Some of the tribe's chiefs signed a treaty which gave the Cheyenne a small triangular piece of land to live on. Only 6 of the 44 chiefs signed the treaty, but the U.S. government considered this a binding agreement. One of the chiefs who signed the treaty was Black Kettle. He was presented an American flag and told that as long as he flew this flag over his teepee, he and his people would not be harmed.

Groups of Cheyenne would occasionally leave the reservation and conduct raids against white settlements. It is unclear whether Black Kettle knew or approved of these raids. However, word reached him that a band of Cheyenne raiders had been attacked and killed. In an effort to look into the matter, Black Kettle and another Cheyenne chief, Lean Bear, led a small group to investigate. The U.S. Cavalry spotted them and assumed they were another group of hostile raiders. The cavalrymen opened fire, killing Lean Bear and several others. Black Kettle pleaded for the violence to stop.

Black Kettle negotiated more than once on behalf of his people and was eventually instructed to take his followers to the Sand Creek reservation. He was told that they would be safe there. Almost immediately, Colonel John Chivington was sent to attack the group of "hostile natives". On November 29th, 1864, Colonel Chivington and 700 soldiers charged the Sand Creek encampment while the Cheyenne were still asleep. Men, women, and children were slaughtered. Black Kettle tried to explain that they were peaceful, showing the soldiers the flying American flag he was given, as well as a white flag, the traditional symbol for surrender. The soldiers ignored these symbols though.

Following the Sand Creek Massacre, many of Black Kettle's followers abandoned him in favor of more warlike leaders. However, shortly after the massacre, he led a small band of followers to Indian Territory. They settled a village on the Washita River, near present-day Cheyenne, Oklahoma.

Words to watch for:
teepee   hostile
massacre   renegade

In this same area, some of Black Kettle's former followers had turned violent. They had conducted raids on white settlements, taking hostages and stealing livestock. Lt. Colonel George Armstrong Custer had been sent out with the 7th Cavalry to deal with the problem.

Custer discovered Black Kettle's encampment on the Washita River. Believing that this was the renegade group they were looking for, Custer and his men attacked. On November 27th, 1868, more than 100 Cheyenne were killed, including Black Kettle and his wife. This incident became known as the Washita Massacre.

Following the death of Black Kettle, many Cheyenne surrendered, ready to give up the fight and move to the reservations in Indian Territory. Black Kettle is remembered today as a peacekeeper who longed to protect his people. His memory is preserved at the Black Kettle Museum in Cheyenne, Oklahoma.

Multiple Choice: *Select the choice that completes the statement or answers the question.*

1._____ Which of the following best explains why the Cheyenne were living on a small triangular piece of land?
a. This was their ancient tribal land that they refused to leave.
b. Six Cheyenne chiefs had signed a treaty which moved the entire tribe to this land.
c. The white settlers moving into this area had forced them onto this land after a bloody battle.
d. There was gold on that piece of land and the Cheyenne refused to surrender it to white settlers.

2._____ Which of the following best summarizes the Sand Creek Massacre?
a. This was a major battle between white settlers and Native Americans that resulted in hundreds of deaths on both sides.
b. A group of Cheyenne warriors surrounded a homestead of white settlers and slaughtered them without provocation.
c. A large group of U.S. soldiers attacked a peaceful camp of Cheyenne while they were sleeping, killing men, women, and children.
d. The Cheyenne were rounded up and forced to march at gunpoint from Colorado to Indian Territory.

3._____ Following the Sand Creek Massacre, Black Kettle took his followers to which of the following locations?
a. a village on the Washita River, outside of present-day Cheyenne, Oklahoma
b. a remote region far to the north in present-day Montana
c. a village on the Red River, near present-day Sherman, Texas
d. a remote region far to the south, just across the Mexican border on the Rio Grande

4._____ George Armstrong Custer and the 7th Cavalry had been sent out to deal with which of the following problems?
a. They were supposed to remove Black Kettle's settlement and tell them to go elsewhere.
b. A herd of wild buffalo had become rabid. Custer had been given instructions to put the herd down.
c. A family of settlers had gone missing. Custer had been instructed to find them and return them to their homestead.
d. A band of Cheyenne was conducting raids on white settlements, taking hostages and stealing livestock.

5._____ Which of the following best describes the Washita Massacre?
a. Custer and all of his men were surrounded and killed after being pursued for several miles.
b. Most of Custer's men were killed, but he managed to escape, returning to Fort Reno.
c. Custer and his men attacked Black Kettle's camp, killing Black Kettle and more than 100 of his followers.
d. A white settlement along the Washita River was surrounded and attacked by Cheyenne warriors, all of the settlers, except a few small children, were killed.

Guided Reading: *Fill in the blanks below to create complete sentences.*

1. The Cheyenne and Arapaho tribes had always kept the peace with white settlers who moved into _____.

2. Even though the Cheyenne were largely _____, many of the settlers felt nervous about their presence.

3. Groups of Cheyenne would occasionally leave the _____ and conduct raids against white settlements.

4. The U.S. Cavalry spotted them, and assumed they were another group of hostile raiders. The cavalrymen opened fire, killing _____ and several others.

5. Black Kettle negotiated more than once on behalf of his people and was eventually instructed to take his followers to the _____ reservation.

6. Black Kettle tried to explain that they were peaceful, showing the soldiers the flying _____ he was given.

7. Following the Sand Creek Massacre, many of Black Kettle's followers abandoned him in favor of more _____ leaders.

8. Some of Black Kettle's former followers had turned _____.

9. Following the death of Black Kettle, many Cheyenne _____, ready to give up the fight and move to the reservations.

10. Black Kettle's memory is preserved at the Black Kettle Museum in _____, Oklahoma.

Vocabulary: *Match each word with its correct definition. Consider how the word is used in the lesson. This might help you define each term. Use a dictionary to help if necessary.*

a. teepee
b. reservation
c. hostile

d. massacre
e. renegade

11._____ a piece of land set aside for a special purpose

12._____ a cone-shaped dwelling, usually made of animal skins, used by certain Native American tribes

13._____ a person who abandons their cause in favor of another

14._____ the unnecessary killing of a large number of human beings or animals

15._____ unfriendly; the opposing side

Summarize: *Answer the following questions in the space provided. Attempt to respond in a complete sentence for each question. Be sure to use correct capitalization and punctuation.*

1. Who was sent to the Sand Creek encampment to attack "hostile natives"?

2. What was Black Kettle told about the American flag he was given?

3. When did the Washita Massacre occur?

4. Where was gold discovered in 1858?

5. Why did the Cheyenne and Arapaho have to continue moving further west?

6. How is Black Kettle remembered today?

Student Response: *Write a paragraph addressing the questions raised below. A thorough response should consist of three to five complete sentences.*

7. Imagine being a member of Black Kettle's encampment during either the Sand Creek or Washita Massacres. Describe the emotions you are feeling as the attack occurs. How would you feel about Black Kettle and his decisions which led to these incidents? Are you mad? Scared? Confused? Explain your answer as thoroughly as possible.

Roman Nose

Not all Cheyenne were as peaceful as Black Kettle. Roman Nose was a Cheyenne warrior who did not accept the idea of western expansion and white settlement. Who was Roman Nose? What was his goal?

Roman Nose hoped to evict the white man from his territory and keep the land free of fences, houses, and railroads. Following the Sand Creek Massacre, Roman Nose became one of the principal figures amongst the Cheyenne.

Roman Nose was never a chief, but his skill on the battlefield was nearly unmatched. He was such an imposing and intimidating figure that some in the U.S. military mistakenly believed that he was the chief of the entire Cheyenne Nation. He stood over six feet tall with a muscular build. Roman Nose was well-known for his combat abilities and fought with a group known as the Dog Soldiers. While he was not officially the leader, he was the accepted leader during conflict.

Throughout the 1860s, the Dog Soldiers became increasingly hostile towards white settlers. They and other Cheyenne refused to sign the treaties that Black Kettle was signing. Instead, they raided settlements and became a major detriment to whites attempting to settle in Colorado.

In 1868, a group of volunteer soldiers from Fort Hays, Kansas was sent out to track down the Cheyenne raiding parties. On September 5th, they began tracking a group of Cheyenne who they believed had killed three people. The soldiers tracked this group for two weeks before making camp at a location known as Beecher Island. What they did not realize was that Roman Nose and a band of Cheyenne warriors had been tracking them as well.

On the morning of September 17th, the soldiers woke to the sounds of war cries as the Cheyenne attacked. The size of the attacking force was unknown, but estimates range anywhere from 200 to 1,000. The Battle of Beecher Island raged for several hours. However, the soldiers were using seven-shot repeating rifles. The attacking war party was demolished. Roman Nose was killed during the battle. Following the death of Roman Nose, many of the Cheyenne were devastated. Their efforts to defend their homelands nearly fell apart over the course of the next year.

Words to watch for:

imposing Dog Soldiers

detriment Roman Nose

Today, Roman Nose is remembered as one of the greatest Cheyenne warriors and an influential figure of the Plains Indian Wars of the 1860s. Even though Roman Nose never lived in the state, he has been honored with Roman Nose State Park in central Oklahoma. This location is near where many of the Cheyenne eventually resettled.

Multiple Choice: *Select the choice that completes the statement or answers the question.*

1._____ Which of the following correctly identifies when Roman Nose became one of the principal figures amongst the Cheyenne?
a.   He inherited this position from his father who died when Roman Nose was still a young warrior.
b.   He became a principal figure after distinguishing himself in battle at Beecher Island.
c.   He became a principal figure of the Cheyenne following the Sand Creek Massacre.
d.   He was elected principal chief of the Cheyenne shortly after the Cheyenne signed their first removal treaty.

2._____ Which of the following most accurately describes Roman Nose?
a.   He was small in stature, but made up for it with a courageous fighting spirit.
b.   He was over six feet tall, with a muscular build, and was an unquestioned leader in combat.
c.   He was soft spoken and peaceful. He tried to avoid fighting at every opportunity.
d.   He was a tribal elder and one of the oldest and wisest men in the entire Cheyenne tribe.

3._____ Which of the following best describes the intention of the volunteer soldiers who left Fort Hays in 1868?
a.   Their intention was to track down a Cheyenne raiding party.
b.   Their intention was to help a group of settlers establish a homestead.
c.   Their intention was to escort a wagon train of food and supplies back to the fort.
d.   Their intention was to find those who were poaching buffalo and bring them to justice.

4._____ Which of the following proved to be the deciding factor in the Battle of Beecher Island?
a.   The sheer numbers of the Cheyenne force overwhelmed the volunteer soldiers.
b.   The leadership ability of Roman Nose tilted the balance in favor of the Cheyenne.
c.   The 7th Cavalry arrived near the end of the battle to allow a victory for the U.S. Army.
d.   The volunteer soldiers were using seven-shot repeating rifles which had a devastating impact.

5._____ Which of the following statements about Roman Nose is not accurate?
a.   He is remembered as one of the most influential figures of the Plains Indian Wars.
b.   Roman Nose State Park in central Oklahoma is named in his honor.
c.   Roman Nose lived in Oklahoma for a brief time towards the end of his life.
d.   Roman Nose hoped to keep his land free of fences, houses, and railroads.

Vocabulary: *Match each word with its correct definition. Consider how the word is used in the lesson. This might help you define each term. Use a dictionary to help if necessary.*

a.   imposing
b.   Dog Soldiers
c.   detriment

d.   Roman Nose
e.   Battle of Beecher Island

6._____   a battle between the U.S. Army and the Cheyenne, at which Roman Nose died

7._____   a militaristic society of aggressive Cheyenne warriors

8._____   a highly-feared Cheyenne war leader in the 1860s

9._____   the cause of a disadvantage; something that causes harm

10._____   very impressive because of its size or appearance

Guided Reading: *Fill in the blanks below to create complete sentences.*

1. Roman Nose was a Cheyenne warrior who did not accept the idea of western
_____.

2. Following the Sand Creek Massacre, Roman Nose became one of the principal figures
amongst the _____.

3. Throughout the 1860s, the _____ became increasingly
hostile towards white settlers.

4. In 1868, a group of volunteer soldiers from _____, Kansas
were sent out to track down the Cheyenne raiding parties.

5. On the morning of September 17th, the soldiers woke to the sounds of
_____ as the Cheyenne attacked.

Correct the Statement: *Each of the following sentences is false. Circle the incorrect word(s) and
write the word or phrase that makes the statement correct in the answer blank provided.*

6. Roman Nose was well-known for his negotiating abilities, and fought with a group
known as the Dog Soldiers. _____.

7. The Dog Soldiers and other Cheyenne refused to sign the treaties that Quanah Parker
was signing. _____.

8. The soldiers tracked this group for two weeks, before making camp at a location
known as Sand Creek. _____.

9. Today, Roman Nose is remembered as one of the greatest Cheyenne holy men.
_____.

10. He has been honored with Roman Nose State Park, in eastern Oklahoma.
_____.

Summarize: *Answer the following questions in the space provided. Attempt to respond in a complete sentence for each question. Be sure to use correct capitalization and punctuation!*

1. Who was signing the treaties that the rest of the Cheyenne refused to sign?

2. What did Roman Nose hope to do?

3. When did the Battle of Beecher Island take place?

4. Where did Roman Nose die?

5. Why did the attacking war party get demolished so quickly (at Beecher Island)?

6. How was Roman Nose thought of by the U.S. military?

Student Response: *Write a paragraph addressing the questions raised below. A thorough response should consist of three to five complete sentences.*

7. The Plains Indian Wars of the mid to late 19th Century made for one of the darkest chapters in American History. Do you feel there was any way this tragedy could have been avoided? Explain your answer as thoroughly as possible.

General Philip Sheridan & Quanah Parker

Two of the legendary figures of the "Indian Wars" were General Philip Sheridan and Quanah Parker. Who were these two men? How did they become so memorable?

General Philip Sheridan was only 5' 5" and weighed 115 pounds. However, during the Civil War he displayed immense amounts of courage that far outweighed his small stature. He distinguished himself at several different battles including Murfreesboro and Chattanooga.

Following the Civil War, Sheridan was given the task of pacifying the plains and bringing the Plains Indian tribes onto reservations in Indian Territory. To do this, he used a strategy of attacking the Cheyenne, Kiowa, Comanche, and other tribes during the winter months. He would take their supplies and livestock, hoping to force them on to the reservations if they hoped to survive.

Sheridan's tactics in dealing with the Plains Indians are often considered brutal. A popular legend regarding Philip Sheridan recounts a meeting between the general and a Comanche chief named Tosawi. Tosawi approached the general and introduced himself by saying, "Me, Tosawi, good Indian." General Sheridan callously replied, "The only good Indians I ever saw were dead."

However, despite his gruff demeanor, he was an extremely influential figure in the Great Plains region. Sheridan established several frontier forts, some of which are still in operation today. Fort Reno, Fort Arbuckle, and Fort Sill were all established by the general.

Words to watch for:

pacifying   callously

demeanor   influential

One of the chiefs that General Sheridan had many dealings with was Quanah Parker. Parker was a member of the Quahada Comanche and served as the principal Chief of the Comanche after they had moved to a reservation in Indian Territory. Starting in 1874, Parker led groups of Comanche and Cheyenne warriors off of the reservation and into Texas. They attacked merchants and buffalo hunters who sought buffalo for their hides (items made of buffalo fur were quite popular at the time). This greatly bothered Parker and other chiefs because the buffalo had always been an important source of food, fuel, clothing, and construction materials for their tribes.

These raids precipitated the Red River War. General Sheridan ordered large numbers of soldiers out to bring an end to the attacks on buffalo hunters. The army scoured the Texas panhandle, searching for the raiding war parties. The Red River War came to a conclusion with the Battle of Palo Duro Canyon. The U.S. Army seized over 1,4000 Comanche horses and destroyed large amounts of buffalo meat. Following this battle, Parker and the other Comanche returned to Fort Sill and surrendered. This represented the end of the free-roaming Native American population on the Great Plains.

Parker lived out the remainder of his life in Oklahoma and became one of the key figures in the Native American Church Movement. He died in 1911 and was buried near Cache, Oklahoma. In 1957, his body was moved to the Fort Sill Post Cemetery where it remains today.

Quanah Parker is remembered in a number of ways. He has had several buildings, as well as an elementary school, named in his honor. Multiple communities have streets named for him, and his home in Cache is listed on the National Register of Historic Places.

Multiple Choice: *Select the choice that completes the statement or answers the question.*

1._____ Which of the following best summarizes the task Philip Sheridan was given after the Civil War?
a.   to rid the plains of all buffalo and any other unwanted pests
b.   to survey the plains and section it off, preparing the land for eventual settlement
c.   pacify the plains and bring the plains tribes onto the reservations in Indian Territory
d.   to make detailed maps and notes of the Great Plains and explore the land thoroughly

2._____ Which of the following best describes General Sheridan's methods of dealing with Native Americans?
a.   His tactics were brutal. He would take their livestock and supplies, forcing them onto the reservations.
b.   He was very gentle. He tried to encourage Native Americans onto the reservations by showing them the positive aspects.
c.   He was a shrewd negotiator. He would often negotiate with Native American chiefs, convincing them that reservation life was their best option.
d.   His tactics were devious. He would trick tribal leaders into signing agreements they did not fully understand.

3._____ Which of the following best summarizes Quanah Parker's interaction with buffalo hunters and merchants?
a.   Parker filed a lawsuit to prevent the buffalo hunters from hunting on tribal grounds.
b.   Parker and his warriors would attack hunters who wanted the buffalo for their hides.
c.   Parker would assist the buffalo hunters, helping them track down herds of buffalo.
d.   Parker and his tribe made hats, coats, and blankets out of the hides that buffalo hunters brought them.

4._____ Which of the following makes the Battle of Palo Duro Canyon significant?
a.   The U.S. Army seized over 1,400 Comanche horses.
b.   The U.S. Army destroyed large amounts of buffalo meat.
c.   Quanah Parker and the other Comanche returned to Fort Sill.
d.   This battle represented the end of the free-roaming Native American population on the Great Plains.

5._____ In which of the following ways has Quanah Parker *not* been recognized?
a.   Parker State Park in southern Oklahoma is named in his honor.
b.   He has had several buildings and an elementary school named in his honor.
c.   There are many communities which have streets named for him.
d.   His home in Cache is listed on the National Register of Historic Places.

Vocabulary: *Match each word with its correct definition. Consider how the word is used in the lesson. This might help you define each term. Use a dictionary to help if necessary.*

a. pacify   d. influential
b. callous   e. scour
c. demeanor

1._____ insensitive; unsympathetic; indifferent

2._____ to search for thoroughly

3._____ something that has great importance

4._____ the way a person behaves towards others

5._____ to restore a state of peace

Guided Reading: *Fill in the blanks below to create complete sentences.*

6. General Philip Sheridan displayed immense amounts of _____ that far outweighed his small stature.

7. Sheridan attacked the Cheyenne, Kiowa, Comanche, and other tribes during the _____ months.

8. Despite his gruff demeanor, Sheridan was an extremely influential figure in the _____ region.

9. One of the chiefs that General Sheridan had many dealings with was _____.

10. Parker was a member of the _____ Comanche.

11. Starting in 1874, Parker led groups of Comanche and Cheyenne warriors off of the reservation and into _____.

12. The _____ War came to a conclusion with the Battle of Palo Duro Canyon.

13. The U.S. Army seized over 1,4000 Comanche _____ and destroyed large amounts of buffalo meat.

14. Parker lived out the remainder of his life in _____ and became one of the key figures in the Native American Church Movement.

15. In 1957, Parker's body was moved to the _____ Post Cemetery.

Summarize: *Answer the following questions in the space provided. Attempt to respond in a complete sentence for each question. Be sure to use correct capitalization and punctuation!*

1. Who was placed in charge of pacifying the Plains Indians?

2. What position did Quanah Parker serve in after the Comanche had been moved to the reservation in Indian Territory?

3. When did the Red River War begin?

4. Where did General Sheridan distinguish himself?

5. Why did the buffalo hunting bother Quanah Parker and his fellow Comanche?

6. Aside from his dealings with plains tribes, how was General Sheridan an influential figure in the Great Plains region?

Student Response: *Write a paragraph addressing the questions raised below. A thorough response should consist of three to five complete sentences.*

7. How do you feel about the buffalo hunting craze of the late 1800s? Should they have hunted the buffalo as they did for only their hide? Or should they have been more protective of the species?

In the years following the Civil War, many Native American tribes in the western region of the United States were relocated to Indian Territory. Utilize a map of the United States or internet resources to help you locate and label the following locations.

Forts should be labeled with a □. Battlefields should be labeled with an X.

| Arizona | Battle of Beecher Island (near Wray, CO) | Roman Nose State Park | Fort Sill |
| New Mexico | Washita Battlefield (near Cheyenne, OK) | Fort Arbuckle | Fort Reno |

Color each labeled state a different color.

The Civil War & Post-War Indian Removal: Post Assessment

Vocabulary: *Match each word with its correct definition.*

a. massacre
b. guerilla
c. Roman Nose
d. pacify

e. teepee
f. reservation
g. Dog Soldiers
h. cavalry

1._____ a piece of land set aside for a special purpose

2._____ a cone-shaped dwelling, usually made of animal skins, used by certain
        Native American tribes.

3._____ a military force composed of soldiers on horseback

4._____ a small armed force that usually depends on hit-and-run tactics

5._____ to restore a state of peace

6._____ a militaristic society of aggressive Cheyenne warriors

7._____ a highly feared Cheyenne warrior of the 1860s

8._____the unnecessary killing of a large number of humans or animals

Multiple Choice: *Select the choice that completes the statement or answers the question.*

9._____ Which of the following was *not* amongst the reasons that many in the tribal
        nations wanted to join the Confederacy?
a. All of the tribes had originally come from Southern states.
b. They shared a similar culture and way of life to those living in Southern states.
c. They felt it was necessary in order to preserve the United States of America.
d. Many still had relatives living in Southern states.

10._____ Which of the following was *not* one of the reasons the Confederacy
        hoped to persuade Indian Territory into joining them?
a. There were herds of cattle that could be used for beef and leather.
b. There were large deposits of lead which could be used for ammunition.
c. The Confederacy hoped to use Indian Territory as a base to set up trade with Mexico.
d. It was hoped that Indian Territory could serve as a buffer zone between Kansas and Texas.

11._____ Which of the following best explains why many Native Americans did not
        want to become involved in the war at all?
a. They saw it as a choice between those who had forced them off of their tribal land and the
   federal government that had allowed them to do it.
b. Native American tribes had always been very peaceful and avoided violence at all costs.
c. The tribes believed that both sides of the conflict were wrong.
d. Most believed that since they were independent nations, they should declare their neutrality
   and wait to sign a trade agreement with the victorious side.

12._____ During the Civil War, who was the Creek leader that established a neutral camp
            at the Deep Fork River?
a. Geronimo   c. Roman Nose
b. Opothleyahola   d. Tecumseh

13._____ Which of the following best explains the significance of the Battle of Honey Springs?
a. General James G. Blunt won a resounding victory, allowing him to move on to greater fame.
b. This was the only battle that was actually fought in Indian Territory throughout the entire war.
c. Fort Smith was captured by Union forces, cutting Indian Territory off from the Arkansas River.
d. It was the first battle in which Native American soldiers played a major role in the fighting.

14._____ Which of the following best describes the type of fighting that Quantrill's Raiders
            became well-known for?
a. They were fierce fighters who were well-known for always being on the frontlines of
    every battle.
b. They were a network of spies that kept their eye on Union troop movements.
c. They were a cavalry unit that frequently supported infantry troops during engagements.
d. They conducted guerilla raids in which they struck targets quickly before disappearing.

15._____ Which of the following best explains why the nation had never settled the regions of
            New Mexico and Arizona?
a. The region was a desert and no one wanted to settle there.
b. The Apache were so fierce that no one dared to settle in the area.
c. The president had outlawed any settlement until the year 1870.
d. The nation had become distracted by the Civil War.

16._____ Which of the following correctly identifies Geronimo's real name?
a. Goyathlay   c. Black Kettle
b. Roman Nose   d. Opothleyahola

17._____ Which of the following best summarizes the efforts to capture Geronimo?
a. Geronimo was tricked into attending a peace conference. When he arrived he was apprehended
    without a struggle.
b. More than 5,000 soldiers attempted to capture Geronimo and his followers throughout the
    1870s and '80s.
c. The pursuit of Geronimo continued for years until the hunt was finally discontinued. Geronimo
    was allowed to live out his life in Arizona.
d. Geronimo briefly evaded capture, but knew his cause was hopeless. He quickly surrendered
    and retired to life in Indian Territory.

18._____ Which of the following accurately describes Geronimo's final years?
a. He lived at Fort Sill in Indian Territory and performed in Wild West shows.
b. He disappeared into the mountains of Mexico, never to be seen again.
c. He was shot and killed by U.S. soldiers in one last, final standoff.
d. He was taken to a prison in Washington D.C. where he lived out his life.

19._____ Which of the following best explains why the Cheyenne were living on a small triangular piece of land?

a. This was their ancient tribal land that they refused to leave.

b. Six Cheyenne chiefs had signed a treaty which moved the entire tribe to this land.

c. The white settlers moving into this area had forced them onto this land after a bloody battle.

d. There was gold on that piece of land and the Cheyenne refused to surrender it to white settlers.

20._____ Which of the following best summarizes the Sand Creek Massacre?

a. This was a major battle between white settlers and Native Americans that resulted in hundreds of deaths on both sides.

b. A group of Cheyenne warriors surrounded a homestead of white settlers and slaughtered them without provocation.

c. A large group of U.S. soldiers attacked a peaceful camp of Cheyenne while they were sleeping, killing men, women, and children.

d. The Cheyenne were rounded up and forced to march at gunpoint from Colorado to Indian Territory.

21._____ Following the Sand Creek Massacre, Black Kettle took his followers to which of the following locations?

a. a village on the Washita River, outside of present-day Cheyenne, Oklahoma

b. a remote region far to the north in present-day Montana

c. a village on the Red River, near present-day Sherman, Texas

d. a remote region far to the south, just across the Mexican border on the Rio Grande

22._____ George Armstrong Custer and the 7th Cavalry had been sent out to deal with which of the following problems?

a. They were supposed to remove Black Kettle's settlement and tell them to go elsewhere.

b. A herd of wild buffalo had become rabid. Custer had been given instructions to put the herd down.

c. A family of settlers had gone missing. Custer had been instructed to find them and return them to their homestead.

d. A band of Cheyenne was conducting raids on white settlements, taking hostages and stealing livestock.

23._____ Which of the following best describes the Washita Massacre?

a. Custer and all of his men were surrounded and killed after being pursued for several miles.

b. Most of Custer's men were killed, but he managed to escape, returning to Fort Reno.

c. Custer and his men attacked Black Kettle's camp, killing Black Kettle and more than 100 of his followers.

d. A white settlement along the Washita River was surrounded and attacked by Cheyenne warriors, all of the settlers, except a few small children, were killed.

24._____ Which of the following proved to be the deciding factor in the Battle of Beecher Island?

a. The sheer numbers of the Cheyenne force overwhelmed the volunteer soldiers.

b. The leadership ability of Roman Nose tilted the balance in favor of the Cheyenne.

c. The 7th Cavalry arrived near the end of the battle to allow a victory for the U.S. Army.

d. The volunteer soldiers were using seven-shot repeating rifles which had a devastating impact.

25._____ Which of the following best summarizes the task Philip Sheridan was given after the Civil War?
a. to rid the plains of all buffalo and any other unwanted pests
b. to survey the plains and section it off, preparing the land for eventual settlement
c. pacify the plains and bring the plains tribes onto the reservations in Indian Territory
d. to make detailed maps and notes of the Great Plains and explore the land thoroughly

26._____ Which of the following best describes General Sheridan's methods of dealing with Native Americans?
a. His tactics were brutal. He would take their livestock and supplies, forcing them onto the reservations.
b. He was very gentle. He tried to encourage Native Americans onto the reservations by showing them the positive aspects.
c. He was a shrewd negotiator. He would often negotiate with Native American chiefs, convincing them that reservation life was their best option.
d. His tactics were devious. He would trick tribal leaders into signing agreements they did not fully understand.

27._____ Which of the following supposedly said, "The only good Indians I ever saw were dead"?
a. George Armstrong Custer
b. Ulysses S. Grant
c. Philip Sheridan
d. Robert E. Lee

28._____ Which of the following best explains why the buffalo hunting bothered Quanah Parker and his fellow Comanche?
a. It bothered them because they were not allowed to share in the profits of the hunting.
b. The army insisted that a certain number of buffalo be killed every single month.
c. The Comanche were being blamed for the hunting that was being done by white hunters.
d. The Comanche used every part of the buffalo for meat, clothing, and other uses.

29._____ Which of the following best summarizes Quanah Parker's interaction with buffalo hunters and merchants?
a. Parker filed a lawsuit to prevent the buffalo hunters from hunting on tribal grounds.
b. Parker and his warriors would attack hunters who wanted the buffalo for their hides.
c. Parker would assist the buffalo hunters, helping them track down herds of buffalo.
d. Parker and his tribe made hats, coats, and blankets out of the hides that buffalo hunters brought them.

30._____ Which of the following makes the Battle of Palo Duro Canyon significant?
a. The U.S. Army seized over 1,400 Comanche horses.
b. The U.S. Army destroyed large amounts of buffalo meat.
c. Quanah Parker and the other Comanche returned to Fort Sill.
d. This battle represented the end of the free-roaming Native American population on the Great Plains.

Completion: *Fill in the blanks below to create complete sentences.*

Colorado   Quanah Parker   Sand Creek   American flag   Apache
reservation   Confederacy   Dog Soldiers   Geronimo   war-like

31. By May of 1861, four of the five tribes had allied themselves with the
_____.

32. Amongst the western tribes that were removed were the Kiowa, Comanche, Cheyenne,
Arapaho, and _____.

33. _____'s battle skills were unmatched and both Mexican and
American settlers were terrified of him.

34. The Cheyenne and Arapaho tribes had always kept the peace with white settlers who moved
into _____.

35. Groups of Cheyenne would occasionally leave the _____ and
conduct raids against white settlements.

36. Black Kettle negotiated more than once on behalf of his people and was eventually instructed
to take his followers to the _____ reservation.

37. Black Kettle tried to explain that they were peaceful, showing the soldiers the flying
_____ he was given.

38. Following the Sand Creek Massacre, many of Black Kettle's followers abandoned him in
favor of more _____ leaders.

39. Throughout the 1860s, the _____ became increasingly hostile
towards white settlers.

40. _____ was a member of the Quahada Comanche.

The Chisholm Trail

The Chisholm Trail became one of the most important cattle trails in America during the 1870s. Where was the Chisholm Trail? Who was it named after?

Jesse Chisholm was born in Tennessee in 1806. His father was Scottish, his mother was Cherokee. He had been a frontier trader nearly his entire life. He was fluent in fourteen different Native American languages. The U.S. government recognized this ability and would occasionally call on Chisholm to help negotiate treaties with different tribes.

Chisholm operated several trading posts on the frontier in the 1850s. One of those trading posts was located near the Red River; another was in Kansas City, Kansas. As a result, Chisholm spent a good deal of time traveling in between the two places. The trail between these two locations became known as the Chisholm Trail.

Following the Civil War, the trail became quite a popular route for cattle ranchers. Large herds of cattle were herded from Texas to the nearest railroad lines, which were in Kansas. From there, the animals would be loaded into boxcars and shipped to eastern states where the beef would command high prices.

The cattle drives that moved along the Chisholm Trail became legendary. Thousands of cattle with each drive would make their way across the Red River and into Indian Territory. Each drive was very similar. Drives usually occurred in the spring or fall, with approximately nine or ten cowboys attempting to maintain control of the herd.

> *Words to watch for:*
>
> *fluent   terrain*
>
> *tributaries stampede*

The cowboys worked for about a dollar a day and lived in fairly rough conditions. There were few baths, if any, and little shelter from the heat or cold. They lived in the dust, dirt, and manure kicked up by the animals they were moving. There were other difficulties as well, including the terrain. The Red River and the Arkansas River both had to be crossed, not to mention countless other smaller streams and tributaries. The cattle themselves were also quite dangerous as stampedes were a constant danger.

Cattle rustlers and Native Americans also created difficulties for the cowboys as they herded cattle along the trail. Many Native American tribes living in Indian Territory demanded 10 cents a head for the animals moving across their land.

The trail ran all the way from the Red River into northern Kansas. Its route through Indian Territory is roughly the same as U.S. Highway 81. The trail helped establish the Oklahoma towns of Duncan, Chickasha, El Reno, Kingfisher, and Enid, amongst many others. The end of the line for most drives was Abilene, Kansas. In some cases, the trail would extend all the way to Kansas City.

No one is quite sure how many cattle were herded along the Chisholm Trail. The best estimates guess anywhere from 1.5 million all the way up to 5 million head of cattle. As the 1800s progressed, the railroad companies built railroads directly into Texas, making the long journey unnecessary. However, the cattle drives on the Chisholm Trail will continue to live on in the hearts and minds of all those who think fondly of the American Old West.

Multiple Choice: *Select the choice that completes the statement or answers the question.*

1._____ Which of the following best explains how the Chisholm Trail came to be named after Jesse Chisholm?
a. Chisholm was the most well-known cattle rancher in Texas; he moved his cattle along the trail regularly.
b. Chisholm was a famous territorial governor, and the trail was named in his honor.
c. Chisholm owned several trading posts and established the trail as he traveled from one to another.
d. Chisholm traveled the trail as an outlaw, hiding in Indian Territory to escape U.S. Marshals.

2._____ Which of these best explains why cattle had to be herded from Texas to Kansas?
a. Kansas was the location of the nearest railroad, which could take the cattle to the East.
b. The people of Kansas were famous beef eaters, but could not raise their own cattle.
c. Kansas was where all the slaughterhouses were. The animals were butchered there, and the meat was shipped to large cities.
d. The people of Kansas were excellent leatherworkers. They produced saddles and boots which were sold across the nation.

3._____ Which of the following statements is inaccurate?
a. The cowboys on a cattle drive worked for about a dollar a day.
b. One of the most common dangers during a drive was being attacked by wild animals.
c. The Red River and Arkansas River both had to be crossed during a cattle drive.
d. Cattle rustlers could create difficulties for the cowboys driving the cattle.

4._____ Which of the following best summarizes the route of the Chisholm Trail?
a. The trail runs along the extreme western edge of Oklahoma and slices diagonally through Kansas.
b. The trail follows the tributaries of the Red and Arkansas Rivers, so that there was always a large water supply for the cattle.
c. The trail had no real defined route. There were many variants of it for each drive.
d. The trail runs from the Red River into northern Kansas, following the route of Highway 81 through Oklahoma.

5._____ Which of the following best explains why the Chisholm Trail was eventually unnecessary?
a. The demand for beef fell sharply as people became more health conscious.
b. Railroad companies eventually built railroads through Texas.
c. Once the highways were built, the cattle could be shipped with trucks.
d. Synthetic leather eliminated the need for real leather products.

Vocabulary: *Match each word with its correct definition. Consider how the word is used in the lesson. This might help you define each term. Use a dictionary to help if necessary.*

a. fluent
b. terrain
c. tributary

d. stampede
e. fond

6._____ having an affection for; cherished

7._____ capable of speaking with ease

8._____ a sudden, frenzied rush of frightened animals

9._____ the physical characteristics of a piece of ground

10._____ a small river that flows into a larger body of water

Guided Reading: *Fill in the blanks below to create complete sentences.*

1. Jesse Chisholm was fluent in _____ different Native American languages.

2. The animals would be loaded into boxcars and shipped to _____ states.

3. The cowboys lived in fairly rough conditions with little shelter from the heat or _____.

4. Native American tribes living in Indian Territory demanded _____ a head for the animals moving across their land.

5. In some cases, the trail would extend all the way to _____.

Correct the Statement: *Each of the following sentences is false. Circle the incorrect word and write the word or phrase that makes the statement correct in the answer blank provided.*

6. One of Jesse Chisholm's trading posts was located near the Arkansas River, another was in Kansas City, Kansas. _____.

7. Following the Mexican War, the trail became quite a popular route for cattle ranchers. _____.

8. Drives usually occurred in the summer or winter, with approximately nine or ten cowboys attempting to maintain control of the herd. _____.

9. The cowboys worked for about five dollars a day. _____.

10. The trail helped establish the Oklahoma towns of Duncan, Shawnee, Kingfisher, and Enid. _____.

Summarize: *Answer the following questions in the space provided. Attempt to respond in a complete sentence for each question. Be sure to use correct capitalization and punctuation!*

1. Who was the Chisholm Trail named after?

2. What are the best estimates of how many cattle were moved on the Chisholm Trail?

3. When did the Chisholm Trail become popular with cattle ranchers?

4. Where did most drives on the Chisholm Trail end?

5. Why were the cattle dangerous?

6. How did Jesse Chisholm assist the U.S. government?

Student Response: *Write a paragraph addressing the questions raised below. A thorough response should consist of three to five complete sentences.*

7. Would you like to have been an old west cowboy working a cattle drive on the Chisholm Trail? Why or why not? Explain your answer as thoroughly as possible.

The Chisholm Trail played an important role in settling several Oklahoma towns. Utilize a map of Oklahoma or internet resources to help you locate and label the following locations.

The trail should be drawn in using red and labeled. Rivers should be drawn in using blue and labeled. Cities and towns should be labeled with a •

Chisholm Trail	Red River	Arkansas River	Duncan
Chickasha	El Reno	Kingfisher	Enid

Belle Starr

One of the most memorable ladies of the Old West was Belle Starr. Who was Belle Starr? How did she become so famous?

Myra Maybelle Shirley was the middle child (and only daughter) of John Shirley. Her father owned a hotel, a bar, a blacksmith shop, and a stable in southwest Missouri. As a result, the Shirley's were quite well-off. Myra grew up in a refined manner. She attended good schools and was taught music and foreign languages. However, she also lived in southwest Missouri with two brothers. She learned how to shoot guns and ride horses, and she loved the outdoors.

During the Civil War, her brother joined Captain William Quantrill's Raiders, and Myra acted as a spy. She would pass on good information to her brother whenever she heard it. Unfortunately, like many others living in Missouri, the war ruined the Shirley's businesses and the family was forced to move to Texas. Myra was miserable in Texas, but one evening, they were visited by Jim Reed. Reed was a friend of her brothers and an outlaw. He needed a place to hide from the authorities.

She and Reed fell in love and the two ran away together, getting married in 1866. The couple traveled the country, living in Missouri, California, and then Texas, always trying to stay one step ahead of the law. The two became involved in several illegal activities, including cattle rustling and counterfeiting. In an effort to evade capture, Myra changed her name to Maybelle and the couple moved to Indian Territory.

In November of 1873, Jim and Maybelle stole $30,000 from a family. Maybelle participated in this robbery while disguised as a man. Not long after this, Maybelle left her husband, believing he had been unfaithful to their marriage vows. She then married a man named Sam Starr (who had once been a business partner with her former husband). At this point, Myra Maybelle changed her name again, and she became forever known as Belle Starr.

The new couple made their home in Indian Territory, near the Canadian River. This location was just about twenty miles away from a cave known as Robber's Roost, or Robber's Cave. While there, the Starr's became notorious for harboring famous outlaws. Jesse James, the Younger Brothers, and many others that history has forgotten found safety from the authorities with the Starrs.

> *Words to watch for:*
>
> stable   evade
>
> harboring infatuated

In 1882, the Starrs sold several horses that didn't belong to them. As a result, Belle was charged with horse theft and sent to prison for nine months. This became the only crime she was ever charged with or convicted of. However, there were almost certainly other criminal deeds. For example, it is believed that she and Sam robbed the U.S. Mail in 1886. Once again, she participated in this crime while dressed in disguise as a man.

Belle's adventures came to an end in 1889. Her home was in the Cherokee Nation, and the Cherokee had instructed her that she could no longer harbor outlaws if she hoped to keep her land. This forced her to turn away Tom Watson, an outlaw who had wanted to live on her land. Watson was furious, and as a result, he shot Belle just after she left a party one evening (although, this was never officially proven).

Fiction writers of the era became infatuated with her name. These writers took Belle Starr and turned her into "the bandit queen", a beautiful, seductive outlaw who rode the range and robbed banks. This fictional portrayal of Belle has helped her name live on throughout the years.

Belle's grave is just southeast of Porum, Oklahoma, and Robber's Cave State Park is opened to the public, just outside of Wilburton, Oklahoma.

©Reading Through History

Multiple Choice: *Select the choice that completes the statement or answers the question.*

1._____ Which of the following best describes Belle Starr's early life?
a. Her family was well-off. She attended good schools and was raised in a refined manner.
b. Her family had little money. She was forced to work several jobs and did not attend school.
c. Her father was a doctor, but they were not wealthy. Her upbringing was similar to most that lived in the mid-1800s.
d. Her father died when she was very young, and her mother was forced to raise the children on her own.

2._____ Which of the following best summarizes Belle Starr's activities during the Civil War?
a. She joined the Union Army, disguised as a man, and served for a year before being discovered.
b. She worked as a nurse in a Confederate hospital, tending to wounded soldiers.
c. She acted as a spy for Quantrill's Raiders, passing along information to her brother.
d. She joined the Women's Defense League, the first all-female regiment in the U.S.

3._____ Which of the following best describes Belle Starr's criminal activity?
a. Belle robbed many banks, always being able to make a daring escape on her horse.
b. Belle participated in several robberies, usually dressed in disguise as a man.
c. Belle was a bloodthirsty killer who always shot first and asked questions later.
d. Belle did not participate in any crimes, but reaped the rewards of her husband's criminal ways.

4._____ Which of the following reasons best explains why Robber's Cave is significant?
a. This was a spot where famous outlaws would hide the loot they stole over the years.
b. This was a spot where fugitives and outlaws were harbored from the authorities.
c. This was a spot where outlaws would take a vow to protect one another from harm.
d. This was the spot where Belle Starr was gunned down and also laid to rest.

5._____ Which of the following has helped Belle Starr's reputation as an outlaw?
a. A biography was written about Belle's life and it brought her to the public's attention.
b. A newspaper columnist followed Belle on many of her adventures and wrote about his journey.
c. Following her death, her stash of loot was discovered at Robber's Cave, creating quite a sensation.
d. Fiction writers of the era turned Belle into "the bandit queen", a beautiful, seductive outlaw.

Vocabulary: *Match each word with its correct definition. Consider how the word is used in the lesson. This might help you define each term. Use a dictionary to help if necessary.*

a. stable
b. counterfeit
c. evade
d. harbor
e. infatuated

6._____ foolishly obsessed with another

7._____ to conceal or hide; to shelter

8._____ a building used for feeding horses

9._____ to escape through trickery or cleverness

10._____ to create a fake version of another item

Guided Reading: *Fill in the blanks below to create complete sentences.*

1. Myra Maybelle Shirley lived in southwest Missouri where she learned how to shoot _____ and ride horses.

2. During the Civil War, her brother joined Captain William Quantrill's _____.

3. The two became involved in several illegal activities, including cattle _____ and counterfeiting.

4. In November of 1873, Jim and Maybelle stole _____ from a family.

5. The new couple made their home in Indian Territory, just about twenty miles away from a cave known as _____.

6. The Starr's became notorious for harboring famous outlaws including _____, the Younger Brothers, and many others.

7. In 1882, the Starrs sold several horses that didn't belong to them and Belle was charged with _____.

8. The _____ had instructed Belle that she could no longer harbor outlaws if she hoped to keep her land.

9. _____ writers of the era became infatuated with Belle Starr's name.

10. Belle's grave is just southeast of _____, Oklahoma.

Summarize: *Answer the following questions in the space provided. Attempt to respond in a complete sentence for each question. Be sure to use correct capitalization and punctuation!*

1. Who (is believed to have) shot Belle Starr?

2. What was the only crime Belle Starr was ever charged with or convicted of?

3. When did Belle Starr die? (What year did it happen?)

4. Where is Robber's Cave State Park?

5. Why was Tom Watson furious at Belle Starr?

6. How did Belle Starr commit most of her criminal activities?

Student Response: *Write a paragraph addressing the questions raised below. A thorough response should consist of three to five complete sentences.*

7. Why do you suppose writers of the era were so fascinated by Belle Starr? Was it her name, or the fact that she was a female outlaw, or something else? Explain your answer as thoroughly as possible.

David Payne & the Boomer Movement

The Boomer Movement played a crucial part in the efforts to settle the unassigned lands. Who were the Boomers? How did the movement start?

In the center of Indian Territory, there was a two million acre piece of land that was not owned by any tribe. It was understood to be public lands, and many believed that they should be allowed to settle there. These lands came to be known as the Unassigned Lands.

There were many people interested in opening the Unassigned Lands (as well as the rest of Indian Territory) to non-Native Americans. The railroad industry was eager to build railroads through the region. The railroad would mean towns springing up along the tracks, and new towns meant new businesses. The banking industry could envision many new business owners needing loans for start-up costs and the construction of new buildings. Of course, there were also thousands of farmers desperate for their own piece of land.

> *Words to watch for:*
>
> notion   escorted
>
> *propaganda confiscated*

The railroad industry began hiring promoters to popularize the notion of settling the Unassigned Lands. One of these promoters was Elias C. Boudinot. Boudinot was the son of Elias Boudinot, one of the Cherokee who had signed the Treaty of New Echota, which led to the eventual Cherokee settlement in Indian Territory.

Elias C. Boudinot published an article in the *Chicago Times* on February 17, 1879. This article claimed that there were millions of acres of valuable farmland in the middle of Indian Territory, just waiting to be claimed by settlers. The article was read by millions of people and generated real interest in these Unassigned Lands.

One man who read this article was David Payne. Payne had spent much time in southern Kansas and explored much of current-day Oklahoma. He was very familiar with the area, having worked as a hunter, scout, soldier, and guide. In the spring of 1879, Payne started organizing colonies of those who sought to settle the Unassigned Lands. The would-be settlers started gathering in Kansas border towns such as Arkansas City, Caldwell, and Hunnewell.

Payne made his first attempt to settle the territory in 1880. He and his followers, who were being called the Boomers, even began construction of a town near the present-day site of Oklahoma City. They were arrested by the U.S. Cavalry and escorted back to Kansas. Payne and the Boomers made several more attempts to settle the Unassigned Lands, and each time they were apprehended by the cavalry and escorted back to Kansas.

In between trips, he would continue expanding the Boomer Movement by giving speeches and recruiting more Boomers. He even published a newspaper, the *Oklahoma War Chief*, which printed Boomer propaganda material. As Payne continued to agitate the situation, the U.S. Army became more aggressive towards him. At one point, soldiers even burned many of his buildings and confiscated his printing press.

Payne died from heart failure on November 27, 1884. His funeral was held in Wellington, Kansas and was attended by thousands of Boomers who mourned his loss. He was never allowed to settle in the Unassigned Lands. However, in 1995, his remains were moved to Stillwater, Oklahoma, the county seat of Payne County, which is named in his honor.

The efforts of Elias C. Boudinot, David Payne, and the Boomers brought the issue of the Unassigned Lands to the nation's attention. The president and Congress realized that they were going to have to act soon and allow this land to be settled.

Multiple Choice: *Select the choice that completes the statement or answers the question.*

1._____ Which of the following statements is inaccurate?
a.   The railroad industry was eager to build new railroads through the unassigned lands.
b.   The banking industry could envision new business owners needing loans for start-up costs.
c.   The Native Americans living in Indian Territory were excited about the potential of new settlers.
d.   Thousands of farmers were desperate for their own piece of land.

2._____ Which of the following best describes what Elias C. Boudinot did to popularize the idea of settling the Unassigned Lands?
a.   He published an article in the *Chicago Times* describing the Unassigned Lands.
b.   He wrote the song "This Land is Your Land" as a way of generating interest.
c.   He traveled the country, giving speeches to large crowds about the territory.
d.   He personally met with the president, insisting that the territory be opened for settlement.

3._____ Which of the following best describes the Boomers?
a.   The Boomers were those who attempted to sneak into the Unassigned Lands just before the land run to stake claims.
b.   The Boomers were a religious cult that followed the teachings of David Payne and were hoping to find a paradise in the Unassigned Lands.
c.   The Boomers were an elite group of soldiers assigned to protect the Unassigned Lands.
d.   The Boomers were a group who tried to establish settlements in the Unassigned Lands, but were repeatedly turned back by the U.S. Army.

4._____ Which of the following did David Payne *not* do to promote the Boomer Movement?
a.   He gave speeches in an effort to recruit more Boomers.
b.   He made several trips with Boomers attempting to settle the Unassigned Lands.
c.   He started a newspaper called the *Oklahoma War Chief*.
d.   He petitioned to the principal chiefs of each of the Five Civilized Tribes.

5._____ Which of the following best summarizes the significance of Elias C. Boudinot and David Payne's efforts?
a.   They became the first settlers in the Unassigned Lands and established Oklahoma City.
b.   Their efforts brought the issue of the Unassigned Lands to the nation's attention.
c.   They became legendary figures of farmers' rights and started the Populist Party.
d.   Their efforts were in vain and the region known as the Unassigned Lands remained unsettled for decades.

Vocabulary: *Match each word with its correct definition. Consider how the word is used in the lesson. This might help you define each term. Use a dictionary to help if necessary.*

a.   notion
b.   escort
c.   propaganda
d.   agitate
e.   confiscate

6._____ to disturb or excite emotionally

7._____ to seize or take away

8._____ information deliberately spread to help or harm a person or cause

9._____ to accompany another for their protection or guidance

10._____ an idea or concept, sometimes of a fanciful nature

Guided Reading: *Fill in the blanks below to create complete sentences.*

1. In the center of Indian Territory, there was a _____ acre piece of land that was not owned by any tribe.

2. The railroad industry began hiring _____ to popularize the notion of settling the Unassigned Lands.

3. Elias C. Boudinot's article was read by millions of people, and it generated real interest in these _____.

4. In the spring of 1879, David Payne started organizing _____ of those who sought to settle the Unassigned Lands.

5. As Payne continued to agitate the situation, the _____ became more aggressive towards him.

Correct the Statement: *Each of the following sentences is false. Circle the incorrect word and write the word or phrase that makes the statement correct in the answer blank provided.*

6. There were many people interested in opening the Unassigned Lands (as well as the rest of Indian Territory) to Native Americans. _____

7. Elias C. Boudinot was the father of Elias Boudinot, one of the Cherokee who had signed the Treaty of New Echota. _____.

8. Elias C. Boudinot's article claimed that there were millions of acres of worthless farmland in the middle of Indian Territory. _____.

9. The would-be settlers started gathering in Texas border towns such as Arkansas City, Caldwell, and Hunnewell. _____

10. David Payne's funeral was held in Wellington, Kansas, and it was attended by hundreds of Boomers who mourned his loss. _____.

Summarize: *Answer the following questions in the space provided. Attempt to respond in a complete sentence for each question. Be sure to use correct capitalization and punctuation.*

1. Who was the leader of the Boomer Movement?

2. What was the title of the newspaper David Payne started?

3. When did Elias C. Boudinot's article appear in the Chicago Times?

4. Where did the Boomer colonies start to form?

5. Why did thousands of farmers want to settle in the Unassigned Lands?

6. How was David Payne so familiar with the region?

Student Response: *Write a paragraph addressing the questions raised below. A thorough response should consist of three to five complete sentences.*

7. Do you feel that the Boomers should have been allowed to settle in the Unassigned Lands, or do you feel this land should have been preserved for Native Americans? Explain your answer as thoroughly as possible.

The Land Run

The Land Run of 1889 was like nothing the world had ever seen before. What was the land run? How did this event take place?

According to the Homestead Act, originally passed in 1862, anyone who was at least twenty-one years of age and the head of a household could claim 160 acres of public land. The homesteader had to agree to live on the land, make improvements, and farm the land for at least five years. It was this law that the Boomers used as their justification for attempting to settle in the Unassigned Lands.

Legal battles over the Unassigned Lands continued for years, as many Native Americans felt that it should continue to be a part of Indian Territory. However, with the passage of the Springer Amendment in early March of 1889, all Native American rights to those lands were given up for $2.25 million. President Benjamin Harrison, who had only been in office for three weeks, issued a proclamation on March 23, 1889. All those eligible under the conditions of the Homestead Act would be allowed to enter the Unassigned Lands on April 22, 1889.

Settlers waiting for the land run

President Harrison's proclamation created great excitement all over the nation. The Boomers had been advocating settlement of this territory for more than ten years, and now the fruits of their labor were becoming a reality. Newspapers and periodicals around the world carried stories about the Unassigned Lands and the great land giveaway that was soon to occur. They referred to the territory as fertile and beautiful, describing it as the "Garden Spot of the World". Thousands of families packed up all of their possessions and headed out towards Indian Territory in hopes of a better life.

> *Words to watch for:*
>
> *homestead   justification*
>
> *proclamation   enterprising*

There were far more homesteaders interested in the land than there were homesteads to be claimed. Therefore, it was determined that all of the land would be given away at once. All prospective settlers would gather around the borders of the Unassigned Lands, but would not be allowed to cross until noon of April 22nd.

As the day approached, the countryside became a sea of Conestoga wagons as the homesteaders arrived in droves. The borders of the Unassigned Lands were heavily guarded by soldiers who were attempting to ensure that no one crossed into the territory prematurely. However, there were some who managed to sneak by these guards and claim land early. These early settlers became known as Sooners.

By Monday, April 22nd, 1889, approximately 50,000 people had gathered around the edges of the Unassigned Lands. Soldiers lined up along the borders, with a gun in one hand and a watch in the other. At precisely noon, each of the soldiers fired their gun, signaling that the race was on.

With a great roar, the crowd rushed across the lines in a mad dash to claim their new homes. Most were on horseback. Typically, the father of the family rode on ahead to secure the homestead while the rest of the family came by wagon at a slower pace. Although, there were other means of transportation used during the land run. Some were in wagons, others rode bicycles, and some even ran on foot!

In just a few hours, nearly all of the sections of land had been claimed. In many cases, the plots had been claimed by more than one person, and it was difficult to determine who had arrived first. Some of these disputes were settled through violence, but most of the time, the matters were resolved peacefully. For example, each homesteader might agree to take 80 acres, rather than the full 160 (although, some of these disputes were taken to court and not decided for several years).

Not everyone who participated in the run was even interested in owning a homestead. Enterprising businessmen recognized that there would be an instant need for general stores, lumber, stage coach services, and many other aspects of modern life. Towns sprung up overnight. Guthrie, Oklahoma City, Kingfisher, and Norman were amongst the largest. It was estimated that Oklahoma City had a population of 12,000 on its first day of existence.

The Land Run of 1889 was merely the first in a series of similar land runs over the course of the next four years. The U.S. government eventually negotiated with eighteen different Native American tribes to acquire their tribal lands in Indian Territory. As each piece was acquired, it was given away.

The biggest and most spectacular of all the land runs occurred on September 16, 1893. The piece of land being given away was known as the Cherokee Outlet. Over 100,000 people participated and more than 6 million acres of land were claimed that day.

By the mid-1890s, the western half of Indian Territory was now being called Oklahoma Territory and Oklahoma was rapidly on its way towards statehood.

Multiple Choice: *Select the choice that completes the statement or answers the question.*

1._____ Which of the following is not true of the Homestead Act?
a. Anyone 21 years of age, and the head of a household, could claim 160 acres of public land.
b. The homesteader had to agree to grow the types of crops that were needed.
c. The homesteader had to agree to live upon the land for five years.
d. The homesteader had to agree to make improvements to the land and farm it.

2._____ Which of the following best summarizes President Benjamin Harrison's proclamation regarding the Unassigned Lands?
a. The Unassigned Lands will become forbidden territory on March 23, 1889, never to be settled by non-Native Americans.
b. All those eligible under the conditions of the Dawes Allotment Act will be given a piece of the Unassigned Lands.
c. The Unassigned Lands will be distributed evenly amongst the Five Civilized Tribes, and they may do with it as they see fit.
d. All those eligible under the conditions of the Homestead Act will be allowed to enter the Unassigned Lands on April 22, 1889.

3._____ Which of the following best summarizes how the Unassigned Lands would be given away?
a. All the lands would be given away in the form of a lottery, with names being selected one at a time.
b. All the lands would be sold in an auction, with each plot of land going to the highest bidder.
c. All the lands would be given away at the same time, with participants lining up around the border of the territory.
d. All the lands would be assigned to prospective homesteaders alphabetically, by last name.

4._____ Which of the following statements about the April 22, 1889 land run is inaccurate?
a. Approximately 500,000 people participated.
b. Most of those attempting to claim land were on horseback.
c. Nearly all of the sections of land had been claimed within a few hours.
d. Some disputes over who had claimed land first were settled through violence.

5._____ Which of the following statements about the Land Run of 1889 is accurate?
a. There were more plots of land than there were people to claim them.
b. Guthrie, Oklahoma City, Kingfisher, and Norman were established during the run.
c. Everyone participating in the run was attempting to claim a homestead.
d. The Land Run of 1889 was the last of the major land runs in Oklahoma Territory.

Vocabulary: *Match each word with its correct definition. Consider how the word is used in the lesson. This might help you define each term. Use a dictionary to help if necessary.*

a. homestead   d. premature
b. justification   e. enterprising
c. proclamation

6._____ a reason or explanation; defense

7._____ occurring too soon

8._____ ready to embark on a new venture; imaginative and bold

9._____ an official and public announcement

10._____ a piece of land with a dwelling and other buildings

Guided Reading: *Fill in the blanks below to create complete sentences.*

1. The _____ were attempting to use the Homestead Act as their justification for trying to settle in the Unassigned Lands.

2. Newspapers and periodicals around the world carried stories about the Unassigned Lands and the great _____ that was soon to occur.

3. The borders of the Unassigned Lands were heavily guarded by _____ who were attempting to ensure that no one crossed into the territory prematurely.

4. At precisely _____, each of the soldiers fired their gun, signaling that the race was on.

5. Over _____ people participated in the land run for the Cherokee Outlet.

History Word Builder: *Match each historical term with its appropriate definition.*

a. Unassigned Lands
b. Homestead Act
c. Conestoga Wagon
d. Sooners
e. Cherokee Outlet

6._____ a large covered wagon used for transporting families and their belongings

7._____ a law which stated that all those over 21, and the head of a household, could claim 160 acres of public land

8._____ a 6 million acre tract of land in northwest Oklahoma that was once owned by the Cherokee Nation

9._____ a piece of land in the middle of Indian Territory that did not belong to one particular tribe

10._____ land run participants who crossed the border and attempted to claim land prematurely

Summarize: *Answer the following questions in the space provided. Attempt to respond in a complete sentence for each question. Be sure to use correct capitalization and punctuation!*

1. Who issued a proclamation that the Unassigned Lands would be given away?

2. What were some of the businesses started by those who weren't trying to claim land?

3. When did the first land run occur?

4. Where was the biggest and most spectacular land run?

5. Why did some participants only take an 80 acre plot of land instead of 160?

6. How were newspapers and periodicals describing the Unassigned Lands?

Student Response: *Write a paragraph addressing the questions raised below. A thorough response should consist of three to five complete sentences.*

7. Imagine being a participant in the land run in the moments just before, during, and just after the land run had begun. Describe the emotions, sounds, smells, and other sensations that you might be experiencing. Use as much descriptive detail as possible, and use extra paper if necessary.

There were many exciting things happening in Indian Territory during the 1880s and 1890s. Utilize a map of Oklahoma and internet resources to help you locate and label the following places which are mentioned in this unit. Suggested search terms might include "Unassigned Lands" or "Unassigned Territory".

Cities and towns should be labeled with a •   State parks should be labeled with a □

Wilburton	Robber's Cave State Park	
Kingfisher	Norman	Cherokee Outlet	Guthrie
	Unassigned Lands	Oklahoma City

Shade the Unassigned Lands and Cherokee Outlet different colors.

Life on the Prairie

Life was not easy for those who settled on the Great Plains in the late 1800s. These settlers were attempting to take a barren wilderness and turn it into a thriving agricultural area. What did they do to survive? How did they succeed?

The existence of prairie settlers could best be described as one of survival. Shelter was a major concern for most families. At first, the average family might have lived in a tent until a more permanent structure could be built. Unfortunately, there was little wood to be found on the Great Plains, so settlers used whatever they could find. In many cases, sod was the only material available.

Sod houses were made of long strips of dirt, stacked on top of each other. Eventually, the sod would dry and form a solid wall. The walls of a sod house were often very thick, and windows were rare, meaning the homes were dark, with little moving air.

Sod homes were also rather small. Families of five or more might be confined to a dwelling with only one or two rooms. The roof of the home might be a thatched roof made of hay or grass, or perhaps, even more sod. Sod homes were very susceptible to rain damage and required a large amount of maintenance.

Planting and raising crops produced a different set of problems. The prairies they were farming had never been plowed before. The prairie grasses had deep roots that made cultivation nearly impossible.

Settlers raised what they needed, and what they couldn't raise, they would often get by bartering with their neighbors (who might be several miles away). A family with flour might trade some of that flour for butter. Salt might be exchanged for coffee or sugar. Perhaps a settlement with chickens could exchange eggs for milk from a family that had a cow. Fortunately, there were many sources of meat on the plains. Turkey, prairie chickens, pheasant, deer, and other wild game could all be found.

Once supplies were obtained, there was still an issue of cooking the food. There were few trees on the Great Plains, so wood supplies were low. Homesteaders would use whatever they could find as fuel for their fires. One of the most common substitutes was buffalo and cattle manure. Buffalo had been wandering the plains for years, and there seemed to be an inexhaustible supply of manure.

Families would go on expeditions across the countryside, collecting as much as they could find. This was especially true as the winter months approached. The droppings would be used to heat their homes as well as cooking their food. It would not have been an uncommon sight to see each sod dwelling with an enormous pile of manure outside their home.

Words to watch for:

barren   susceptible

barter   substitute

This was a difficult life for many of the settlers. Most were not used to the frontier. They were city-dwellers who were poor, and had no other option but risk everything and settle in such an untamed land. They were used to city life, with stores that had food and clothing.

However, most of these settlers did manage to succeed. They not only survived, but they thrived, and eventually built communities that would prosper.

Multiple Choice: *Select the choice that completes the statement or answers the question.*

1._____ Which of the following best describes the construction of a sod house?
a. A sod house was made of prairie grasses that had been weaved together.
b. A sod house was largely made of animal skins stitched closely together.
c. A sod house was made of long strips of dirt stacked on top of each other.
d. A sod house was a small one room house made of logs and other wood.

2._____ Which of the following statements is inaccurate?
a. Sod houses were usually dark, with little moving air.
b. Sod houses were very comfortable and sturdy structures.
c. Sod houses often had thatched roofs made of hay or grass.
d. Sod houses were susceptible to rain damage.

3._____ Which of the following statements *best* explains why manure was used as fuel for
        homesteader fires?
a. There seemed to be an inexhaustible supply of it.
b. Homesteaders discovered that it burned slower than wood.
c. There were very few trees, which meant wood supplies were low.
d. This was a method that had been recommended by the government.

4._____ Which of the following best explains why life was so difficult for many settlers?
a.   Many were poor city-dwellers who were not used to life on the frontier.
b.   The settlers were frequently attacked by Native Americans who were trying to scare them away.
c.   The government agreed to allow them to settle the land, but refused to provide any assistance.
d.   The land they had settled was a barren desert, unfit for growing crops or sustaining animal life.

5._____ Which of the following statements is not true of frontier life?
a. Families of five or more were often confined to a one room dwelling.
b. Families would often barter what they had, in exchange for what they needed.
c. There were not many sources for meat on the plains.
d. Settlers would go on expeditions to collect manure.

Vocabulary: *Match each word with its correct definition. Consider how the word is used in the lesson. This might help you define each term. Use a dictionary to help if necessary.*

a. barren   d. barter
b. sod   e. substitute
c. susceptible

6._____ unproductive; not producing worthwhile results

7._____ liable to be afflicted by; easily affected by

8._____ a replacement for

9._____ to trade or exchange

10._____ a piece of ground, usually still covered with grass and roots

Guided Reading: *Fill in the blanks below to create complete sentences.*

1. At first, the average family might have lived in a _____ until a more permanent structure could be built.

2. The walls of a sod house were often very _____.

3. Sod homes required a large amount of _____.

4. The prairies that they were farming had never been _____ before.

5. Settlers raised what they needed, and what they couldn't raise, they would often get by _____ with their neighbors.

6. A settlement with chickens could exchange _____ for milk from a family that had a cow.

7. Homesteaders would use whatever they could find as _____ for their fires.

8. The droppings would be used to heat their _____ as well as cooking their food.

9. They were used to city life, with stores that had food and
_____.

10. Most of the settlers did manage to _____.

Summarize: *Answer the following questions in the space provided. Attempt to respond in a complete sentence for each question. Be sure to use correct capitalization and punctuation!*

1. Who would settlers often barter with?

2. What were sod homes made of?

3. When might a family go on a manure collecting expedition?

4. Where might the neighbors be on the frontier?

5. Why was cultivation of the prairie fields nearly impossible?

6. How many rooms did a sod house usually have?

Student Response: *Write a paragraph addressing the questions raised below. A thorough response should consist of three to five complete sentences.*

7. Do you think you could have survived life on the prairie? Why or why not? What would have been the hardest part for you personally, living on the plains? Explain your answer as thoroughly as possible.

Oklahoma has always been famous for its Great Plains region. However, despite the reputation of being "flat", the state boasts many mountain ranges and hilly areas. Utilize a map of Oklahoma and internet resources to help you locate and label the following topographical features.

Mountains should be labeled with the ^^^^^^ symbol.

Glass Mountains	Arbuckle Mountains	Quartz Mountains
Wichita Mountains	Antelope Hills	Osage Hills
	Ouachita Mountains	
	Cookson Hills	

Shade each mountain range or hill region a different color.

Statehood

There were many steps that Oklahoma took along the road to statehood. What were those steps? How long did the process take?

One of the first steps on the road towards statehood was passage of the Dawes Allotment Act, also known as the Dawes Severalty Act. It was created by Senator Henry Dawes of Massachusetts, and its stated goal was to stimulate the assimilation of Native Americans into mainstream American society. The Act authorized the president to survey tribal lands in Indian Territory and divide it into individual allotments. These allotments would then be given to all Native Americans living on those lands. The Dawes Act was initially passed in 1887, and the work of redistributing tribal lands would continue all the way up through 1906 as the government negotiated this process with various tribes. Many Native Americans disagreed with this process because they did not believe in the private ownership of land. However, some were forced to accept allotments of land, whether they wanted it or not.

In 1890, another important step was taken towards statehood. That year, the Oklahoma Organic Act organized the western half of Indian Territory into Oklahoma Territory. The Unassigned Lands also became a part of the new Oklahoma Territory. Throughout the1890s, Oklahoma Territory continued to grow as each piece of tribal land was negotiated for and then given away to settlers through a land run. By the early 1900s, there were two territories in existence. The western half of the current state was known as Oklahoma Territory, while the eastern half was still known as Indian Territory.

There had been many efforts to create a state in this region before. The idea had been proposed since the 1860s. There had been more than a dozen efforts at creating an official territory with proposed names such as Lincoln or Neosho. It wasn't until the late 1880s when the name "Oklahoma" was finally chosen. This was a Choctaw word which literally meant "Land of the Red Man" and was first suggested in 1866. However, it was not officially approved until 1890.

Words to watch for:
allotment   assimilation
obstacles   heritages

There were many obstacles that needed to be overcome before statehood could be achieved. First, Indian Territory had long hoped to be its own state, independent of Oklahoma Territory. At one point, Indian Territory had even held a statehood convention. Known as the Sequoyah Convention, their intention was to create a Native American state known as Sequoyah (named after the legendary Cherokee).

Many on both sides did not feel that the two territories belonged together. Over the course of time, they had developed two very different cultures and ways of life. The people who lived in each territory had come from very different backgrounds and had different heritages.

However, the U.S. Congress was determined to resist all attempts at individual statehood for each territory. Congress was insistent that the two halves would become one state. Those in favor of this suggested that it made more sense to have one strong, healthy state, rather than two weak ones. It would also be roughly the same size (in both population and land) as Kansas and Nebraska. Additionally, the two sides complimented each other. Indian Territory had a wealth of minerals and other natural resources, while Oklahoma Territory had excellent farmland.

Finally, after much debate and many negotiations, the Oklahoma Enabling Act was passed in 1906. This act stated that Oklahoma could begin the work of writing a state constitution. The state constitution was written and approved by Congress. It was ratified by the people on September 17, 1907, and it took effect on November 16, 1907. Oklahoma had officially become the 46th state of the United States.

Multiple Choice: *Select the choice that completes the statement or answers the question.*

1._____ Which of the following best summarizes the Dawes Allotment Act?
a.   Tribal lands were surveyed into individual allotments and the allotments were given to all Native Americans living on those lands.
b.   Tribal lands were forcibly taken away from the tribes and given to non-Native American homesteaders.
c.   The act called for a series of land runs to take place, which gave away all tribal lands to non-Native American homesteaders.
d.   Tribal lands were removed from settlement consideration and declared secure for the next fifty years.

2._____ Which of the following best explains why many Native Americans disagreed with the Dawes Allotment process?
a.   Native Americans had been promised that their tribal lands would never be a part of the United States.
b.   Many Native Americans did not believe in private ownership of property.
c.   Most Native Americans had no desire to live next to white settlers.
d.   Native Americans did not want the land they were living on; they were still fighting to win back their native lands in the South.

3._____ The word "Oklahoma" means which of the following?
a.   "Land of the Great Plains"   c.   "Land of Many Lakes"
b.   "Land of the Rolling Hills"   d.   "Land of the Red Man"

4._____ Which of the following is *not* one of the reasons why Congress wanted Indian Territory and Oklahoma Territory to become one state?
a.   It was better to have one healthy state than two weak ones.
b.   The new state would be roughly the same size as its neighbor states.
c.   Congress had negotiated an agreement with the eastern states which limited the number of western states that would join the Union.
d.   The two territories complimented each other well, with each providing different resources.

5._____ Which of the following statements is inaccurate?
a.   The Oklahoma Enabling Act was passed in 1907.
b.   The Oklahoma Enabling Act stated that Oklahoma could begin writing a state constitution.
c.   The state constitution was ratified by the people on September 17, 1907.
d.   The state constitution went into effect on November 16, 1907.

Vocabulary: *Match each word with its correct definition. Consider how the word is used in the lesson. This might help you define each term. Use a dictionary to help if necessary.*

a.   allotment   d.   stimulate
b.   assimilation   e.   heritage
c.   obstacle

6._____ a way of life and history passed down from one generation to the next

7._____ a portion of something given to one individual or group

8._____ to rouse into action; encourage

9._____ something that stands in the way, or hinders progress

10._____ the merging of distinct cultural groups into one

Guided Reading: *Fill in the blanks below to create complete sentences.*

1. The Dawes Allotment Act authorized the president to survey _____ lands in Indian Territory and divide it into individual allotments.

2. The Oklahoma Organic Act organized the western half of Indian Territory into _____ Territory.

3. There had been more than a dozen efforts at creating an official territory, with proposed names such as _____ or Neosho.

4. Native Americans wanted to create a Native American state known as _____.

5. The _____ was determined to resist all attempts at individual statehood for each territory.

Correct the Statement: *Each of the following sentences is false. Circle the incorrect word(s) and write the word or phrase that makes the statement correct in the answer blank provided.*

6. The Unassigned Lands also became a part of the new Indian Territory. _____.

7. The western half of the current state was known as Oklahoma Territory, while the eastern half was still known as Sequoyah Territory. _____.

8. It wasn't until the early 1900s when the name "Oklahoma" was finally chosen. _____.

9. Over the course of time, the two territories had developed two very similar cultures and ways of life. _____.

10. The new state would also be roughly the same size (in both population and land) as Montana and Nebraska. _____.

Summarize: *Answer the following questions in the space provided. Attempt to respond in a complete sentence for each question. Be sure to use correct capitalization and punctuation!*

1. Who did they plan on naming the Native American state in honor of?

2. What was the stated goal of the Dawes Allotment Act?

3. When was the name Oklahoma officially approved?

4. Which half of the current state was actually known as Oklahoma Territory?

5. Why did many not feel that the two territories belonged together?

6. How did Oklahoma Territory continue to grow throughout the 1890s?

Student Response: *Write a paragraph addressing the questions raised below. A thorough response should consist of three to five complete sentences.*

7. Do you feel that they made the correct decision by creating one state rather than two? Would it have been better to have two smaller states? Explain your answer as thoroughly as possible, and cite specific textual evidence if applicable.

The Oklahoma State Constitutional Convention

Before Oklahoma could become a state, it was necessary to write a state constitution. How was this achieved? Who wrote this document?

In the United States of America, each territory that desired to become a state was required to adopt a state constitution. In 1906, after the passage of the Oklahoma Enabling Act, the twin territories of Oklahoma Territory and Indian Territory began the process of making a new state constitution a reality.

The first step was to elect delegates who would attend the convention. Fifty-five delegates from each territory, as well as two delegates from the Osage Nation (which had not yet been added to either territory), were selected. Amongst these 112 delegates were 47 farmers, very appropriate for a state well-known for agriculture. There were also 27 lawyers, 12 merchants, 6 preachers, 3 doctors, and 2 teachers in attendance. 100 of the delegates were Democrats and 12 were Republicans.

The convention was dominated by delegates from Indian Territory. The convention president was William H. Murray and the vice-president was Pete Hanraty, both from Indian Territory. Other prominent attendees included Charles Haskell and Henry Johnston, who went on to become governors of the state, and Robert Williams who would later serve as governor and the state's first Chief Justice. Many of the delegates from Indian Territory had attended the Sequoyah Convention just one year before. This was the failed effort to make Indian Territory the state of Sequoyah by itself. Much of the work done at the Sequoyah Convention served as a good foundation for the Oklahoma state constitution.

The Oklahoma state constitution was written during the Progressive Movement. Progressives believed in utilizing the government to correct the problems they observed in society. Progressive ideals were evident throughout the delegates' work. Amongst the Progressive measures included were an eight hour workday in mines and no children under 15 being hired for hazardous occupations. Free public education for all children between the ages of 8 and 16 was also included. Another Progressive cause discussed was the prohibition of alcohol. Alcohol was illegal in Indian Territory, and this was something the Indian Territory delegates were insistent upon. This topic was eventually left to be voted on by the people.

Words to watch for:

constitution foundation

progressive prohibition

When the document was finally completed, the Oklahoma state constitution was ten times longer than the U.S. Constitution. Some, like William Jennings Bryan, felt that it was the best state constitution ever written and a model for other states to use in the future. Others, like President Theodore Roosevelt, thought it was the worst thing he had ever read. In fact, Roosevelt stated that his comments were "not fit for print". However, the constitution was submitted to the people for ratification on September 17, 1907.

That same day, the people of Oklahoma also voted on the prohibition measure, which passed. This meant that alcohol would be illegal in the state of Oklahoma until 1933 (although, prohibition still remained in some communities until 1958!). Oklahomans also elected their first governor, Charles Haskell, as well as their first representatives to Congress on September 17th, 1907.

President Roosevelt signed the statehood proclamation on November 16, 1907. Shortly afterwards, a public announcement was made in Guthrie where several thousand citizens had gathered to await the news. Oklahoma was admitted as the 46th state of the United States of America.

Multiple Choice: *Select the choice that completes the statement or answers the question.*

1._____ Which of the following best explains what each territory had to do before becoming a state?
a. Each territory was required to pledge an oath of allegiance to the nation.
b. Each territory was required to adopt a state constitution.
c. Each territory was required to adopt a state song and a state symbol.
d. Each territory was required to pay a tribute to the national government.

2._____ Which of the following statements about the Oklahoma state constitutional convention is inaccurate?
a. The convention was largely dominated by representatives from Indian Territory.
b. The convention delegates were largely unsure of what kind of constitution their citizens wanted.
c. There were many delegates who would go on to play prominent roles in Oklahoma politics.
d. The work done at the Sequoyah Convention served as a good foundation for the state constitution.

3._____ Which of the following was not one of the Progressive measures included in the Oklahoma state constitution?
a. an eight hour workday in the mines
b. no children under the age of 15 were to be hired for hazardous occupations
c. free public schools for children between the ages of 8 and 16
d. a minimum wage of $2 an hour

4._____ Which of the following statements about the Oklahoma state constitution is inaccurate?
a. The Oklahoma state constitution was ten times longer than the U.S. Constitution.
b. The U.S. Congress refused to pass the first draft of the document.
c. William Jennings Bryan felt that the document should serve as a model for other states.
d. Theodore Roosevelt stated that his thoughts on the document were "not fit for print".

5._____ Which of the following measures did Oklahomans approve the same day they approved the state constitution?
a. a measure which prohibited the sale of alcohol in Oklahoma until 1933
b. a measure which implemented a minimum wage of $2 an hour
c. a measure which made it illegal to hunt wild game until 1950
d. a measure which declared there would be no state income tax until 1935

Vocabulary: *Match each word with its correct definition. Consider how the word is used in the lesson. This might help you define each term. Use a dictionary to help if necessary.*

a. constitution
b. foundation
c. progressive

d. prohibition
e. ratification

6._____ the act of giving formal approval or consent

7._____ a document which states the fundamental principles by which a state is governed

8._____ to forbid or make illegal

9._____ the basis or groundwork for something

10._____ someone who believes in using the government to correct society's problems

Guided Reading: *Fill in the blanks below to create complete sentences.*

1. In 1906, after the passage of the Oklahoma _____ Act, the twin territories of Oklahoma Territory and Indian Territory began the process of making a new state constitution a reality.

2. _____ delegates from each territory, as well as 2 delegates from the Osage Nation, were selected.

3. Amongst these 112 delegates, there were 47 _____.

4. 100 of the delegates were _____ and 12 were Republicans.

5. Prominent attendees included _____ and Henry Johnston, both who went on to become governors.

6. _____ was illegal in Indian Territory, and this was something the Indian Territory delegates were insistent upon.

7. _____ felt that it was the best state constitution ever written.

8. The constitution was submitted to the people for ratification on _____ 17, 1907.

9. Prohibition still remained in some communities until _____!

10. Oklahoma was admitted as the _____ state of the United States of America.

Summarize: *Answer the following questions in the space provided. Attempt to respond in a complete sentence for each question. Be sure to use correct capitalization and punctuation!*

1. Who was the president at the Oklahoma state constitutional convention?

2. What significance did the Sequoyah Convention play in writing the state constitution?

3. When did President Roosevelt sign the statehood proclamation?

4. Where was a public announcement made that the statehood proclamation had been signed?

5. Why were there so many Progressive measures included in the state constitution?

6. How was the issue of prohibition decided?

Student Response: *Write a paragraph addressing the questions raised below. A thorough response should consist of three to five complete sentences.*

7. Examine paragraph three of this lesson more closely. If a new state constitution were written today, what would be different about the occupations of the delegates and the political parties those delegates represented?

The Land Run & Statehood: Post Assessment

Vocabulary: *Match each word with its correct definition.*

a. stampede
b. tributary
c. counterfeit
d. homestead

e. Conestoga wagon
f. harbor
g. propaganda
h. confiscate

1._____ to conceal or hide; to shelter

2._____ to create a fake version of another item

3._____ a sudden frenzied rush of frightened animals

4._____ a small river that flows into a larger body of water

5._____ to seize or take away

6._____ information deliberately spread to help or harm an individual or cause

7._____ a piece of land with a dwelling and other buildings

8._____ a large covered wagon used for transporting families and their belongings

Vocabulary: *Match each word with its correct definition.*

a. progressive
b. barter
c. constitution
d. Homestead Act

e. Sooners
f. ratification
g. Unassigned Lands
h. sod

9._____ a law which stated that all those over 21, and the head of a household, could claim 160 acres of public land

10._____ a piece of land in the middle of Indian Territory that did not belong to any one particular tribe

11._____ land run participants who crossed the border and attempted to claim land prematurely

12._____ to trade or exchange

13._____ a piece of ground, usually still covered with grass and roots

14._____ the act of giving formal approval or consent

15._____ a document which states the fundamental principles by which a state is governed

16._____ someone who believes in using the government to correct society's problems

Multiple Choice: *Select the choice that completes the statement or answers the question.*

17._____ Which of the following correctly identifies who the Chisholm Trail was named after?
a. John Chisholm   c. Frank Chisholm
b. Jesse Chisholm   d. Stanley Chisholm

18._____ Most cattle drives on the Chisholm Trail came to an end in which city?
a. Abilene, KS   c. Enid, OK
b. Kansas City, KS   d. Omaha, NE

19._____ Which of these best explains why cattle had to be herded from Texas to Kansas?
a. Kansas was the location of the nearest railroad, which could take the cattle to the East.
b. The people of Kansas were famous beef eaters, but could not raise their own cattle.
c. Kansas was where all the slaughterhouses were. The animals were butchered there, and the meat was shipped to large cities.
d. The people of Kansas were excellent leatherworkers. They produced saddles and boots which were sold across the nation.

20._____ Which of the following best explains why the Chisholm Trail was eventually unnecessary?
a. The demand for beef fell sharply as people became more health conscious.
b. Railroad companies eventually built railroads through Texas.
c. Once the highways were built, the cattle could be shipped with trucks.
d. Synthetic leather eliminated the need for real leather products.

21._____ Which of the following best describes Belle Starr's criminal activity?
a. Belle robbed many banks, always being able to make a daring escape on her horse.
b. Belle participated in several robberies, usually dressed in disguise as a man.
c. Belle was a bloodthirsty killer who always shot first and asked questions later.
d. Belle did not participate in any crimes, but reaped the rewards of her husband's criminal ways.

22._____ Which of the following reasons best explains why Robber's Cave is significant?
a. This was a spot where famous outlaws would hide the loot they stole over the years.
b. This was a spot where fugitives and outlaws were harbored from the authorities.
c. This was a spot where outlaws would take a vow to protect one another from harm.
d. This was the spot where Belle Starr was gunned down and also laid to rest.

23._____ Which of the following has helped Belle Starr's reputation as an outlaw?
a. A biography was written about Belle's life and it brought her to the public's attention.
b. A newspaper columnist followed Belle on many of her adventures and wrote about his journey.
c. Following her death, her stash of loot was discovered at Robber's Cave, creating quite a sensation.
d. Fiction writers of the era turned Belle into "the bandit queen", a beautiful, seductive outlaw.

24._____ Which of the following statements is inaccurate?
a. The railroad industry was eager to build new railroads through the unassigned lands.
b. The banking industry could envision new business owners needing loans for start-up costs.
c. The Native Americans living in Indian Territory were excited about the potential of new settlers.
d. Thousands of farmers were desperate for their own piece of land.

25._____ Which of the following correctly identifies the leader of the Boomer Movement?
a. Philip Sheridan
b. Belle Starr
c. William H. Murray
d. David Payne

26._____ Which of the following best describes what Elias C. Boudinot did to popularize the idea of settling the Unassigned Lands?
a. He published an article in the *Chicago Times* describing the Unassigned Lands.
b. He wrote the song "This Land is Your Land" as a way of generating interest.
c. He traveled the country, giving speeches to large crowds about the territory.
d. He personally met with the president, insisting that the territory be opened for settlement.

27._____ Which of the following best describes the Boomers?
a. The Boomers were those who attempted to sneak into the Unassigned Lands just before the land run to stake claims.
b. The Boomers were a religious cult that followed the teachings of David Payne and were hoping to find a paradise in the Unassigned Lands.
c. The Boomers were an elite group of soldiers assigned to protect the Unassigned Lands.
d. The Boomers were a group who tried to establish settlements in the Unassigned Lands, but were repeatedly turned back by the U.S. Army.

28._____ Which of the following did David Payne *not* do to promote the Boomer Movement?
a. He gave speeches in an effort to recruit more Boomers.
b. He made several trips with Boomers attempting to settle the Unassigned Lands.
c. He started a newspaper called the *Oklahoma War Chief.*
d. He petitioned to the principal chiefs of each of the Five Civilized Tribes.

29._____ Which of the following best summarizes the significance of Elias C. Boudinot and David Payne's efforts?
a. They became the first settlers in the Unassigned Lands and established Oklahoma City.
b. Their efforts brought the issue of the Unassigned Lands to the nation's attention.
c. They became legendary figures of farmers' rights and started the Populist Party.
d. Their efforts were in vain and the region known as the Unassigned Lands remained unsettled for decades.

30._____ Which of the following is not true of the Homestead Act?
a. Anyone 21 years of age, and the head of a household, could claim 160 acres of public land.
b. The homesteader had to agree to grow the types of crops that were needed.
c. The homesteader had to agree to live upon the land for five years.
d. The homesteader had to agree to make improvements to the land and farm it.

31._____ Which of the following best summarizes President Benjamin Harrison's proclamation regarding the Unassigned Lands?
a. The Unassigned Lands will become forbidden territory on March 23, 1889, never to be settled by non-Native Americans.
b. All those eligible under the conditions of the Dawes Allotment Act will be given a piece of the Unassigned Lands.
c. The Unassigned Lands will be distributed evenly amongst the Five Civilized Tribes, and they may do with it as they see fit.
d. All those eligible under the conditions of the Homestead Act will be allowed to enter the Unassigned Lands on April 22, 1889.

32._____ Which of the following best summarizes how the Unassigned Lands would be
given away?
a.   All the lands would be given away in the form of a lottery, with names being selected one at a time
b.   All the lands would be sold in an auction, with each plot of land going to the highest bidder.
c.   All the lands would be given away at the same time, with participants lining up around the border
of the territory.
d.   All the lands would be assigned to prospective homesteaders alphabetically, by last name.

33._____ Which date correctly identifies when the first land run occurred?
a. April 19, 1922   c. April 5, 1865
b. April 22, 1889   d. April 1, 1900

34._____ Which of the following correctly identifies the 6 million acre tract of land in
Northwest Oklahoma that was once owned by the Cherokee?
a. Cherokee Prairie   c. Cherokee Outlet
b. Cherokee Plains   d. Cherokee Oasis

35._____ Which of the following statements is inaccurate?
a. Sod houses were usually dark, with little moving air.
b. Sod houses were very comfortable and sturdy structures.
c. Sod houses often had thatched roofs made of hay or grass.
d. Sod houses were susceptible to rain damage.

36._____ In the early days of settlement, why was the cultivation of prairie fields nearly
impossible?
a. Settlers lacked the proper tools to cultivate land.
b. Torrential rains made plowing fields difficult.
c. The soil had never been plowed before.
d. A severe drought had made the ground extremely hard.

37._____ Which of the following best summarizes the Dawes Allotment Act?
a.   Tribal lands were surveyed into individual allotments and the allotments were given to all
Native Americans living on those lands.
b.   Tribal lands were forcibly taken away from the tribes and given to non-Native American
homesteaders.
c.   The act called for a series of land runs to take place, which gave away all tribal lands to
non-Native American homesteaders.
d.   Tribal lands were removed from settlement consideration and declared secure for the next
fifty years.

38._____ Which of the following best explains why many Native Americans disagreed with
the Dawes Allotment process?
a.   Native Americans had been promised that their tribal lands would never be a part of the
United States.
b.   Many Native Americans did not believe in private ownership of property.
c.   Most Native Americans had no desire to live next to white settlers.
d.   Native Americans did not want the land they were living on; they were still fighting to win back
their native lands in the South.

39._____ The word "Oklahoma" means which of the following?
a. "Land of the Great Plains"   c. "Land of Many Lakes"
b. "Land of the Rolling Hills"   d. "Land of the Red Man"

40._____ Which of the following is *not* one of the reasons why Congress wanted Indian
              Territory and Oklahoma Territory to become one state?
a. It was better to have one healthy state than two weak ones.
b. The new state would be roughly the same size as its neighbor states.
c. Congress had negotiated an agreement with the eastern states which limited the number of
    western states that would join the Union.
d. The two territories complimented each other well, with each providing different resources.

41._____ Which of these men was president of the Oklahoma Constitutional Convention?
a. William H. Murray   c. Wiley Post
b. Will Rogers   d. Woody Guthrie

42._____ Which of the following statements about the Oklahoma state constitutional
              convention is inaccurate?
a. The convention was largely dominated by representatives from Indian Territory.
b. The convention delegates were largely unsure of what kind of constitution their citizens wanted.
c. There were many delegates who would go on to play prominent roles in Oklahoma politics.
d. The work done at the Sequoyah Convention served as a good foundation for the state constitution.

Completion: *Fill in the blanks below to create complete sentences.*

| 100,000 | Enabling | 46th | bartering |
| Unassigned Lands | Sequoyah | Democrats | noon |

43. Elias C. Boudinot's article was read by millions of people, and it generated real interest in the
_____.

44. At precisely _____, each of the soldiers fired their gun, signaling that the
race was on.

45. Over _____ people participated in the land run for the Cherokee Outlet.

46. Settlers raised what they needed, and what they couldn't raise, they would often get by
_____ with their neighbors.

47. Native Americans wanted to create a Native American state known as
_____.

48. In 1906, after the passage of the Oklahoma _____ Act, the twin
territories of Oklahoma Territory and Indian Territory began the process of making a new state
constitution a reality.

49. One hundred of the delegates were _____ and 12 were
Republicans.

50. Oklahoma was admitted as the _____ state of the United States of America.

Early History through Statehood: Post Assessment

Multiple Choice: _Select the choice that completes the statement or answers the question._

1._____ Which of the following best summarizes the earliest native settlers in Oklahoma?
a. The earliest settlers were farmers who raised beans, squash, sunflowers, and tobacco.
b. The earliest settlers were nomadic wanderers who hunted big game like the wooly mammoth.
c. The earliest settlers were French fur trappers who trapped raccoons and beaver.
d. The earliest settlers were Spanish conquistadors who believed there was gold in the area.

2._____ Which of the following best describes the Spiro Mounds?
a. The Spiro Mounds were made of cedar logs covered with dirt. They were used for religious temples and burial mounds.
b. The Spiro Mounds were constructed of bricks and mortar. They were used as housing by ancestors of the Caddo.
c. The Spiro Mounds were supposedly made of solid gold. Although many archaeologists have searched for them, the mounds have never been found.
d. The Spiro Mounds were made entirely of ivory. They were used strictly as burial chambers for wealthy tribe members.

3._____ Which of the following best summarizes how Coronado treated the Native Americans he encountered?
a. He had little respect for the natives, forcing them to carry his equipment while robbing them of their food.
b. Coronado was very friendly towards the natives and traded many items with them.
c. Coronado attempted to be friendly, but was chased away by the Native Americans who attacked him.
d. Coronado did not encounter any Native Americans during his expedition.

4._____ Which of the following correctly identifies Coronado's guide as he traveled throughout the Southwest?
a. The Turk   c. Sacajawea
b. Pocahontas   d. Squanto

5._____ Which of the following best summarizes the purpose of Juan Padilla's expedition?
a. Padilla was searching for the Seven Cities of Cíbola.
b. Padilla was searching for the Fountain of Youth.
c. Padilla was attempting to Christianize the Wichita Indians.
d. Padilla was attempting to locate the source of the Red River.

6._____ Which of the following accurately summarizes the notes LaHarpe made about his journey?
a. He noted that the Wichita were unfriendly, the area was virtually devoid of wildlife, and that the land was a barren desert.
b. He noted that there was little water, very few trees, and it was not fit for human habitation.
c. He noted that the local natives were very hostile, most of the wildlife was predatory in nature, and overall the territory was a very dangerous place.
d. He noted that the Wichita were excellent farmers, the area was plentiful in wildlife, and the that land was fertile and rich with minerals.

7._____ Which of the following best describes the relationship between the French and Native Americans?
a.   The French were rude to the Native Americans and had a difficult time with them.
b.   The French treated the Native Americans well and established good trade relations.
c.   The French attacked the Native Americans immediately, trying to chase them from the area.
d.   The French did not encounter any Native Americans during their earliest explorations.

8._____ Which of the following best summarizes the purpose of Zebulon Pike's expedition?
a.   He was to find Pike's Peak and climb it.
b.   He was to find the source of the Arkansas and Red Rivers, make detailed maps, and determine the value of natural resources.
c.   He was to find the source of the Mississippi River and establish friendly relationships with Native American tribes.
d.   He was to find deposits of salt and silver, as well search for the mythical cities of gold that Coronado had searched for.

9._____ Which of the following best summarizes the expedition led by Lt. James Wilkinson?
a.   They explored the Arkansas River through the winter months, facing extreme cold and ice.
b.   They explored the Red River through the summer months, facing extreme heat with little water.
c.   They explored the Canadian River through the spring and thought the region was wonderful.
d.   They explored the Arkansas River through the fall months and became hopelessly lost.

10._____ Which of the following significant discoveries did George Sibley make?
a.   He discovered the Sibley Falls, which is the tallest waterfall in North America.
b.   He discovered Sibley Peak, which is the tallest mountain west of the Mississippi River.
c.   He discovered the Great Plains and gave it the nickname "the Great American Desert".
d.   He discovered the Great Salt Plains, "an inexhaustible supply of ready-made salt."

11._____Which of the following correctly identifies the nickname given to present-day Oklahoma as a result of Stephen Long's exploration?
a.   The Vast Wasteland   c.   The Dust Bowl
b.   The Great American Desert   d.   The Great American Prairie

12._____ Which of the following best describes Thomas Nuttall's contribution to exploring the Louisiana Territory?
a.   He was the first to see the Gloss Mountains and gave them their name.
b.   He discovered the source of the Arkansas River and followed it back to the Mississippi.
c.   He located the Great Salt Plains and took extensive notes about the region.
d.   He studied the wide variety of plant and animal life found in the Louisiana Territory.

13._____ Which famous explorer was the first to contact several of the Five Civilized Tribes?
a.   Francisco Coronado   c.   Hernando de Soto
b.   Bernard de LaHarpe   d.   Ponce de Leon

14._____ Which of the following most accurately reflects why little is known about the Cherokee prior to the arrival of European settlers?
a.   The Cherokee are very secretive and do not tell outsiders about their tribal history.
b.   Most of the Cherokee records from that time period were lost in a great fire.
c.   The Cherokee, like other Native American tribes, did not keep written records.
d.   The Cherokee tribe did not exist until very recently.

15._____ Which of the following properly identifies the two competing groups of Cherokee during the Indian Removal process?

a. The white and the red
b. The traditionalists and the progressives
c. The full-bloods and the mixed-bloods
d. The Bear Party and the Moose Party

16._____ Which of the following best summarizes the Treaty of Doak's Stand?

a. The Choctaw agreed to cease all hostilities against the US government.
b. The Choctaw agreed to cede nearly half of their tribal lands to the United states.
c. The Choctaw agreed to pay the United States $3 million to continue living on their tribal lands.
d. The Choctaw agreed to join the United States and enter the Union as the state of Mississippi.

17._____ Which of the following best summarizes the beliefs of Chickasaw and other Native American tribes?

a. Beliefs were passed down in a holy text. This text was strictly adhered to and was read only by tribal elders.
b. Beliefs were learned by memory at an early age. Chickasaw students attended many hours of school to learn all beliefs before they could join society.
c. Beliefs were passed down orally in the form of stories. These stories were usually about animals and had different meanings depending on the tribe.
d. The Chickasaw had no major belief system. Tribal elders determined issues of right and wrong on an independent basis.

18._____ Which of the following best describes what happened to the Mississippian culture?

a. There was a major war between the Mississippian tribes and they were wiped out.
b. The Mississippian tribes mutually agreed to disband and join other tribes.
c. The Mississippian tribes were nearly wiped out by diseases they had no immunity to.
d. There was a major disagreement over who should be the next leader, causing a split.

19._____ The Creek are also known by which of the following names?

a. Iroquois
b. Mississippi
c. Red Sticks
d. Muscogee

20._____ The Seminole tribe was almost exclusively located in which state?

a. Mississippi
b. Georgia
c. Alabama
d. Florida

21._____ Which of the following best summarizes how African slaves began to intermingle with the Seminole?

a. The Seminole purchased slaves from slave traders, just as their neighbors in Georgia did.
b. Slaves escaping from Georgia would intermarry with the tribe.
c. At some point in their distant past, the Seminole had journeyed to Africa.
d. The Seminole were introduced to slavery as part of their assimilation into European American culture.

22._____ Which of the following best explains the significance of the Green Corn Ceremony?

a. The ceremony represented the coming of the new year. It was associated with the return of summer and the ripening of the corn.
b. The ceremony represented the passing of the old year. It was associated with the return of fall and the harvesting of the corn.
c. The ceremony represented the return of new life and was associated with the coming of spring.
d. The ceremony represented the death of elders and was associated with the onset of winter.

23._____ Which of the following best explains why land owned by the
Five Civilized Tribes was in high demand amongst white settlers?
a. All of their tribal lands were near the coast. This land was highly valuable for overseas trading.
b. All of their tribal lands were near major rivers. These waterways were important for shipping, as well as sources of freshwater.
c. The tribal lands were known to be in spots that would not be severely impacted by natural disasters such as tornadoes and hurricanes.
d. Quality farmland that was rich in minerals was becoming increasingly scarce as more settlers moved into the region.

24._____ Why did the Creek not recognize the Treaty of Indian Springs as legitimate?
a. The treaty had been signed by a different tribe, not the Creek.
b. The treaty had been signed by a chief who did not represent the entire tribe.
c. The treaty had not been signed and dated in the official manner.
d. The treaty had already been nullified by the Supreme Court.

25._____ Which of the following best describes the significance of the
Indian Removal Act of 1830?
a. The United States abandoned its efforts to remove Native Americans from their lands and allowed the tribes live in peace.
b. The official policy of the United States became the assimilation of Native Americans into mainstream culture.
c. The official policy of the United States became removing Native Americans from their tribal lands and into Indian Territory.
d. The United States began its effort to locate a piece of land in South America where Native Americans could live in peace.

26._____ Why did the Supreme Court decide that it could not make a ruling in
Cherokee Nation v. Georgia?
a. The Cherokee had not filed the proper paperwork, so their claim was invalid.
b. The state of Georgia had already negotiated a binding contract with the Cherokee.
c. The Supreme Court could only rule on cases involving two different states.
d. The Cherokee Nation was neither an independent nation nor were they citizens of the U.S.

27._____ Which of these most accurately describes the law Georgia passed in an effort to
make life difficult for the Cherokee?
a. Any U.S. citizen living on Cherokee lands had to apply for a license to do so.
b. No citizen of the Cherokee Nation could apply for employment in the state of Georgia.
c. All Cherokee were to report to internment camps and remain there until further notice.
d. The Cherokee were subject to much higher rates of taxation than white citizens.

28._____ Who was Samuel Worcester?
a. He was the highest ranking Chief of the Cherokee Nation.
b. He was the US ambassador who negotiated with the Cherokee.
c. He was a missionary who refused to get a license to live on Cherokee lands.
d. He was a gold prospector who fought to live on Cherokee lands.

29._____ In *Worcester v. Georgia*, the Supreme Court ruled which of the following?
a. The Court ruled that Georgia must return all lands to the Cherokee and pay them reparations for the wrongs committed.
b. The Court ruled that the state of Georgia was perfectly within its rights to force the Cherokee from their lands.
c. The Court ruled that Worcester could not have a case heard in court because he was not a US citizen.
d. The Court ruled that it was the federal government's responsibility to negotiate with Native American tribes.

30._____ Which president is famously quoted as saying, "John Marshall's made his decision; now let him enforce it."
a. Abraham Lincoln
b. George Washington
c. Andrew Jackson
d. James Madison

31._____ Which of the following is most significant about the Treaty of New Echota?
a. The treaty was signed by Major Ridge, John Ridge, and Elias Boudinot.
b. This was the first removal treaty signed by any of the Five Civilized Tribes.
c. This was the last of the major removal treaties signed by the Five Civilized Tribes.
d. The treaty required the Cherokee Nation to cede all of its lands in the Southeast.

32._____ Who was the principal chief of the Cherokee during the removal process?
a. Sequoyah
b. Major Ridge
c. Elias Boudinot
d. John Ross

33._____ Which of the following best summarizes the Cherokee journey on the Trail of Tears?
a. Most of the journey was conducted with wagons or on horseback. It was largely a smooth transition from Georgia to Indian Territory.
b. The Cherokee were rounded up and packed into trains. They were then shipped hundreds of miles to Indian Territory.
c. Most of the journey was on foot and during winter. Outbreaks of diseases, lack of food, and the harsh conditions resulted in thousands of deaths.
d. The Cherokee traveled by boat, through the Gulf of Mexico and up the Mississippi and Arkansas Rivers to arrive in Indian Territory.

34._____ Which of the following best explains what happened to those who signed the Treaty of New Echota?
a. Those who signed the treaty were viewed as heroes and became the new leaders of the Cherokee.
b. Those who signed the treaty were viewed as traitors and executed.
c. Those who signed the treaty had their titles stripped from them and were forced to move out of the tribe.
d. Those who signed the treaty were forced to make a public apology to other tribal members.

35._____ Which of the following made fighting the Seminole in Florida more dangerous?
a. Soldiers would frequently get trapped in quicksand which was difficult to see.
b. The soldiers were frequently dehydrated because of the humid conditions.
c. A mysterious, unknown plague was ravaging the soldiers, leaving many dead.
d. Mosquitos carried malaria which frequently caused death.

36._____ Which of the following best describes how Osceola was captured?
a.   He was deceived into attending peace negotiations and was taken away by soldiers.
b.   He was ambushed in a swamp and surrounded by soldiers.
c.   He was betrayed by one of his top men who told the army of his location.
d.   He surrendered willingly, after being told that his family was being held hostage.

37._____ Why did Major Ridge support the idea of the Cherokee moving west of the
            Mississippi River?
a.   He had traveled to Indian Territory and truly believed it was better land.
b.   He felt it was the best way to preserve the Cherokee way of life and culture.
c.   He would personally receive a large sum of money from the government.
d.   He believed that there was gold in Indian Territory which he hoped to find.

38._____ Which of the following occupations did Elias Boudinot have?
a.   He was principal chief of the Cherokee.
b.   He was a missionary who worked closely with the Cherokee.
c.   He was the Cherokee representative to the U.S. Congress.
d.   He was the editor of the *Cherokee Phoenix*.

39._____ Which of the following best describes what Sequoyah began attempting to do in
            about 1809?
a.   Sequoyah began attempting to create a new type of metal by blending existing metals.
b.   Sequoyah began devising a written system for the Cherokee language.
c.   Sequoyah began to negotiate with the U.S. government, trying to save Cherokee tribal lands.
d.   Sequoyah began construction of a flying machine, but did not complete the work before he died.

40._____ How did John Ross help to change the relationship between Native
            Americans and the U.S. government?
a.   He signed the first removal treaty, which signaled the beginning of the Indian
     Removal process.
b.   He openly challenged the U.S. Army, declaring war between the United States and
     Native Americans.
c.   He appealed directly to the U.S. Congress and helped Native Americans become
     active defenders of their land.
d.   He negotiated a deal with the United States, guaranteeing that all tribes would be compensated
     for their tribal lands.

41._____ Which of the following best summarizes Stand Watie's actions at the outbreak of the
            Civil War?
a.   He volunteered his services to the Confederacy and formed a Native American regiment known
     as the Cherokee Mounted Rifles.
b.   He volunteered his services to the Union and was immediately given the rank of brigadier general.
c.   He sold all of his property and left the country as quickly as he could. He lived in Mexico
     throughout the war and returned after it was over.
d.   He wrote a letter to the leader of both sides, encouraging them to end the violence before it
     destroyed the nation that he loved.

42._____ Which of the following best describes Stand Watie's actions at the conclusion of the Civil War?
a. He returned to the United States and made a fortune off of rebuilding destroyed Southern cities.
b. He became the last Confederate general to surrender in June of 1865.
c. He helped negotiate the peace agreement between the Union and the Confederacy.
d. He refused to surrender, continuing to fight the war for several more years after its conclusion.

43._____ Which of the following was *not* amongst the reasons that many in the tribal nations wanted to join the Confederacy?
a. All of the tribes had originally come from Southern states.
b. They shared a similar culture and way of life to those living in Southern states.
c. They felt it was necessary in order to preserve the United States of America.
d. Many still had relatives living in Southern states.

44._____ Which of the following was *not* one of the reasons the Confederacy hoped to persuade Indian Territory into joining them?
a. There were herds of cattle that could be used for beef and leather.
b. There were large deposits of lead which could be used for ammunition.
c. The Confederacy hoped to use Indian Territory as a base to set up trade with Mexico.
d. It was hoped that Indian Territory could serve as a buffer zone between Kansas and Texas.

45._____ Which of the following best explains why many Native Americans did not want to become involved in the war at all?
a. They saw it as a choice between those who had forced them off of their tribal land and the federal government that had allowed them to do it.
b. Native American tribes had always been very peaceful and avoided violence at all costs.
c. The tribes believed that both sides of the conflict were wrong.
d. Most believed that since they were independent nations, they should declare their neutrality and wait to sign a trade agreement with the victorious side.

46._____ Which of the following best explains the significance of the Battle of Honey Springs?
a. General James G. Blunt won a resounding victory, allowing him to move on to greater fame.
b. This was the only battle that was actually fought in Indian Territory throughout the entire war.
c. Fort Smith was captured by Union forces, cutting Indian Territory off from the Arkansas River.
d. It was the first battle in which Native American soldiers played a major role in the fighting.

47._____ Which of the following best describes the type of fighting that Quantrill's Raiders became well-known for?
a. They were fierce fighters who were well-known for always being on the frontlines of every battle.
b. They were a network of spies that kept their eye on Union troop movements.
c. They were a cavalry unit that frequently supported infantry troops during engagements.
d. They conducted guerilla raids in which they struck targets quickly before disappearing.

48._____ Which of the following best summarizes the efforts to capture Geronimo?
a. Geronimo was tricked into attending a peace conference. When he arrived he was apprehended without a struggle.
b. More than 5,000 soldiers attempted to capture Geronimo and his followers throughout the 1870s and '80s.
c. The pursuit of Geronimo continued for years until the hunt was finally discontinued. Geronimo was allowed to live out his life in Arizona.
d. Geronimo briefly evaded capture, but knew his cause was hopeless. He quickly surrendered and retired to life in Indian Territory.

49._____ Which of the following best summarizes the Sand Creek Massacre?
a. This was a major battle between white settlers and Native Americans that resulted in hundreds of deaths on both sides.
b. A group of Cheyenne warriors surrounded a homestead of white settlers and slaughtered them without provocation.
c. A large group of U.S. soldiers attacked a peaceful camp of Cheyenne while they were sleeping, killing men, women, and children.
d. The Cheyenne were rounded up and forced to march at gunpoint from Colorado to Indian Territory.

50._____ Following the Sand Creek Massacre, Black Kettle took his followers to which of the following locations?
a. a village on the Washita River, outside of present-day Cheyenne, Oklahoma
b. a remote region far to the north in present-day Montana
c. a village on the Red River, near present-day Sherman, Texas
d. a remote region far to the south, just across the Mexican border on the Rio Grande

51._____ Which of the following best describes the Washita Massacre?
a. Custer and all of his men were surrounded and killed after being pursued for several miles.
b. Most of Custer's men were killed, but he managed to escape, returning to Fort Reno.
c. Custer and his men attacked Black Kettle's camp, killing Black Kettle and more than 100 of his followers.
d. A white settlement along the Washita River was surrounded and attacked by Cheyenne warriors, all of the settlers, except a few small children, were killed.

52._____ Which of the following best summarizes the task Philip Sheridan was given after the Civil War?
a. to rid the plains of all buffalo and any other unwanted pests
b. to survey the plains and section it off, preparing the land for eventual settlement
c. pacify the plains and bring the plains tribes onto the reservations in Indian Territory
d. to make detailed maps and notes of the Great Plains and explore the land thoroughly

53._____ Which of the following best describes General Sheridan's methods of dealing with Native Americans?

a. His tactics were brutal. He would take their livestock and supplies, forcing them onto the reservations.

b. He was very gentle. He tried to encourage Native Americans onto the reservations by showing them the positive aspects.

c. He was a shrewd negotiator. He would often negotiate with Native American chiefs, convincing them that reservation life was their best option.

d. His tactics were devious. He would trick tribal leaders into signing agreements they did not fully understand.

54._____ Which of the following best explains why the buffalo hunting bothered Quanah Parker and his fellow Comanche?

a. It bothered them because they were not allowed to share in the profits of the hunting.

b. The army insisted that a certain number of buffalo be killed every single month.

c. The Comanche were being blamed for the hunting that was being done by white hunters.

d. The Comanche used every part of the buffalo for meat, clothing, and other uses.

55._____ Which of the following makes the Battle of Palo Duro Canyon significant?

a. The U.S. Army seized over 1,400 Comanche horses.

b. The U.S. Army destroyed large amounts of buffalo meat.

c. Quanah Parker and the other Comanche returned to Fort Sill.

d. This battle represented the end of the free-roaming Native American population on the Great Plains.

56._____ Which of the following correctly identifies who the Chisholm Trail was named after?

a. John Chisholm   c. Frank Chisholm
b. Jesse Chisholm   d. Stanley Chisholm

57._____ Most cattle drives on the Chisholm Trail came to an end in which city?

a. Abilene, KS   c. Enid, OK
b. Kansas City, KS   d. Omaha, NE

58._____ Which of these best explains why cattle had to be herded from Texas to Kansas?

a. Kansas was the location of the nearest railroad, which could take the cattle to the East.

b. The people of Kansas were famous beef eaters, but could not raise their own cattle.

c. Kansas was where all the slaughterhouses were. The animals were butchered there, and the meat was shipped to large cities.

d. The people of Kansas were excellent leatherworkers. They produced saddles and boots which were sold across the nation.

59._____ Which of the following reasons best explains why Robber's Cave is significant?

a. This was a spot where famous outlaws would hide the loot they stole over the years.

b. This was a spot where fugitives and outlaws were harbored from the authorities.

c. This was a spot where outlaws would take a vow to protect one another from harm.

d. This was the spot where Belle Starr was gunned down and also laid to rest.

60._____ Which of the following correctly identifies the leader of the Boomer Movement?

a. Philip Sheridan   c. William H. Murray
b. Belle Starr   d. David Payne

61._____ Which of the following best describes what Elias C. Boudinot did to popularize the idea of settling the Unassigned Lands?
a. He published an article in the *Chicago Times* describing the Unassigned Lands.
b. He wrote the song "This Land is Your Land" as a way of generating interest.
c. He traveled the country, giving speeches to large crowds about the territory.
d. He personally met with the president, insisting that the territory be opened for settlement.

62._____ Which of the following best describes the Boomers?
a. The Boomers were those who attempted to sneak into the Unassigned Lands just before the land run to stake claims.
b. The Boomers were a religious cult that followed the teachings of David Payne and were hoping to find a paradise in the Unassigned Lands.
c. The Boomers were an elite group of soldiers assigned to protect the Unassigned Lands.
d. The Boomers were a group who tried to establish settlements in the Unassigned Lands, but were repeatedly turned back by the U.S. Army.

63._____ Which of the following best summarizes the significance of Elias C. Boudinot and David Payne's efforts?
a. They became the first settlers in the Unassigned Lands and established Oklahoma City.
b. Their efforts brought the issue of the Unassigned Lands to the nation's attention.
c. They became legendary figures of farmers' rights and started the Populist Party.
d. Their efforts were in vain and the region known as the Unassigned Lands remained unsettled for decades.

64._____ Which of the following is *not* true of the Homestead Act?
a. Anyone 21 years of age, and the head of a household, could claim 160 acres of public land.
b. The homesteader had to agree to grow the types of crops that were needed.
c. The homesteader had to agree to live upon the land for five years.
d. The homesteader had to agree to make improvements to the land and farm it.

65._____ Which of the following best summarizes how the Unassigned Lands would be given away?
a. All the lands would be given away in the form of a lottery, with names being selected one at a time.
b. All the lands would be sold in an auction, with each plot of land going to the highest bidder.
c. All the lands would be given away at the same time, with participants lining up around the border of the territory.
d. All the lands would be assigned to prospective homesteaders alphabetically, by last name.

66._____ Which of the following correctly identifies those who attempted to sneak into the Unassigned Lands just before the land run and stake claims.
a. Boomers   c. Sooners
b. Jayhawks   d. Sidewinders

67._____ Which date correctly identifies when the first land run occurred?
a. April 19, 1922   c. April 5, 1865
b. April 22, 1889   d. April 1, 1900

68._____ Which of the following correctly identifies the 6 million acre tract of land in Northwest Oklahoma that was once owned by the Cherokee?
a. Cherokee Prairie   c. Cherokee Outlet
b. Cherokee Plains   d. Cherokee Oasis

69._____ Which of the following statements is inaccurate?
a. Sod houses were usually dark, with little moving air.
b. Sod houses were very comfortable and sturdy structures.
c. Sod houses often had thatched roofs made of hay or grass.
d. Sod houses were susceptible to rain damage.

70._____ In the early days of settlement, why was the cultivation of prairie fields nearly
            impossible?
a. Settlers lacked the proper tools to cultivate land.
b. Torrential rains made plowing fields difficult.
c. The soil had never been plowed before.
d. A severe drought had made the ground extremely hard.

71._____ Which of the following best summarizes the Dawes Allotment Act?
a. Tribal lands were surveyed into individual allotments and the allotments were given to all
   Native Americans living on those lands.
b. Tribal lands were forcibly taken away from the tribes and given to non-Native American
   homesteaders.
c. The act called for a series of land runs to take place, which gave away all tribal lands to
   non-Native American homesteaders.
d. Tribal lands were removed from settlement consideration and declared secure for the next
   fifty years.

72._____ Which of the following best explains why many Native Americans disagreed with
            the Dawes Allotment process?
a. Native Americans had been promised that their tribal lands would never be a part of the
   United States.
b. Many Native Americans did not believe in private ownership of property.
c. Most Native Americans had no desire to live next to white settlers.
d. Native Americans did not want the land they were living on; they were still fighting to win back
   their native lands in the South.

73._____ Which of the following is *not* one of the reasons why Congress wanted Indian
            Territory and Oklahoma Territory to become one state?
a. It was better to have one healthy state than two weak ones.
b. The new state would be roughly the same size as its neighbor states.
c. Congress had negotiated an agreement with the eastern states which limited the number of
   western states that would join the Union.
d. The two territories complimented each other well, with each providing different resources.

74._____ Which of these men was president of the Oklahoma Constitutional Convention?
a. William H. Murray   c. Wiley Post
b. Will Rogers   d. Woody Guthrie

75._____ Which of the following statements about the Oklahoma Constitutional
            Convention is inaccurate?
a. The convention was largely dominated by representatives from Indian Territory.
b. The convention delegates were largely unsure of what kind of constitution their citizens wanted.
c. There were many delegates who would go on to play prominent roles in Oklahoma politics.
d. The work done at the Sequoyah Convention served as a good foundation for the state constitution.

Answer Key:

Early Native Settlers:
Multiple Choice:

1) B
2) B
3) A
4) D
5) A

Vocabulary:

6) D
7) B
8) A
9) E
10) C

Guided Reading:

1) Wanderers
2) Archaeologists
3) Rabbits
4) Farming
5) Arrows
6) Blankets
7) Chunkey
8) Twelve
9) Looters
10) Spiro, Oklahoma

Summarize:

1. The Spiro Mound builders were ancestors of the Caddo.
2. Foragers collected seeds, nuts, roots, and berries.
3. The Spiro Mounds were excavated in 1933.
4. The first evidence of this tribe's existence was found near Clovis, New Mexico.
5. The Spiro built mounds which had many artifacts in them (OR: Their tribe's existence was much more recent than the other tribes).
6. Cultivation of the ground was done by hand, using sticks and small tools made of stone or perhaps bone.

Student Response:

7. Student answers will vary.

Francisco Coronado & Spanish Exploration:
Multiple Choice:

1) B
2) A
3) D
4) C
5) C

Vocabulary:

6) D
7) A
8) C
9) B
10) E

Guided Reading:

1) Spaniards
2) New Mexico
3) Great Plains
4) Missionary
5) Notes

Correct the Statement:

6) Spain
7) Gold
8) Oklahoma
9) Wichita
10) Juan Padilla

Summarize:

1. The Turk guided Coronado while searching for Quivira.
2. Coronado found adobes that shimmered in the sun like gold from a distance.
3. Coronado and his men left on February 23, 1540.
4. Coronado visited Arizona, New Mexico, Texas, Oklahoma, and Kansas.
5. The Turk was executed for trying to deceive Coronado.
6. Friar Padilla was killed by the Kaw Indians and his followers walked back to Mexico.

Student Response:

7. Student answers will vary.

French Exploration:
Multiple Choice:

1) C
2) A
3) D
4) B
5) C

Guided Reading:

1) French
2) Little Rock
3) Idabel
4) 7,000
5) Fish
6) Gifts
7) Trappers
8) Explorations
9) Town
10) Poteau

Vocabulary:

11) B
12) A
13) E
14) C
15) D

Summarize:

1. Robert de LaSalle named the territory "Louisiana".
2. He gave the local chiefs guns, knives, hatchets, and paint.
3. LaSalle arrived in North America in 1666.
4. The large settlement of Wichita was just south of present-day Tulsa.
5. The French were able to establish a good relationship wit Native Americans because they were treated with them respect and offered them gifts.
6. They made detailed maps and notes which proved helpful to American explorers.

Student Response:

7) Student answers will vary.

American Exploration:
Multiple Choice:

1) B
2) A
3) D
4) B
5) D

Vocabulary:

1) C
2) E
3) B
4) D
5) A

Guided Reading:

6) $15 million
7) source
8) Pike's Peak
9) Spanish
10) boats

Correct the Statement:

11) Osage
12) Arkansas
13) Summer
14) Canadian
15) Botanist

Summarize:

1. Meriwether Lewis & William Clark were sent to explore the northern portion.
2. This region became known as the "Great American Desert".
3. Zebulon Pike's journey began on July 15, 1806.
4. The Big Salt Plain is just outside the present-day town of Freedom, Oklahoma.
5. He felt the area was not fit for settlement because there was little timber and not much surface water.
6. They managed to survive because of friendly Osage Indians that traded with them.

Student Response:

7. Student answers will vary.

Early History Test:

Vocabulary:

1. C
2. F
3. H
4. E
5. G
6. D
7. A
8. B

Multiple Choice:

9. B
10. B
11. C
12. D
13. A
14. A
15. A
16. D
17. A
18. D
19. C
20. B
21. C
22. A
23. D
24. A
25. B
26. C
27. B
28. B
29. D
30. B
31. B
32. D

Completion:

33. Archaeologists
34. New Mexico
35. Great Plains
36. French
37. Explorations
38. Town
39. $15 million
40. Pike's Peak

Cherokee:
Multiple Choice:

1) C
2) D
3) A
4) C
5) C

Vocabulary:

6) D
7) A
8) E
9) B
10) C

Guided Reading:

1) orally
2) Appalachia
3) Hernando de Soto
4) tattooed
5) Civilized
6) confederation
7) traditional
8) European
9) Civil War
10) 300,000

Summarize:

1. The Mixed-Bloods were not in favor of removal, but saw it as inevitable.
2. The red organization was responsible for warfare.
3. The Cherokee adopted a written constitution in the 1820s.
4. The Cherokee Nation's headquarters are in Tahlequah, Oklahoma.
5. They believed they should negotiate, so they could get as much as possible for their land (or, because they believed removal was inevitable).
6. The Cherokee wore bits of cloth, large garments that hung over the entire body, and soft leather moccasins for shoes.

Student Response:

7. Student answers will vary.

Choctaw:
Multiple Choice:

   1)   C
   2)   A
   3)   D
   4)   B
   5)   C

Vocabulary:

   6)   E
   7)   B
   8)   C
   9)   A
   10)   D

Guided Reading:

   1)   Mississippian
   2)   1600s
   3)   Tuskaloosa
   4)   Scotch-Irish
   5)   Baskets
   6)   Lacrosse
   7)   Patrilineal
   8)   Females
   9)   Tribal
   10)   Oklahoma

Summarize:

1. Pushmataha refused to fight against the United States.
2. The Choctaw were forced to sign the Treaty of Doak's Stand in 1820.
3. Tecumseh approached Pushmataha in 1811.
4. The Choctaw originally lived in Louisiana, Mississippi, Alabama, and Florida.
5. They referred to stickball as "little war" because the game could be extremely violent.
6. Pushmataha refused to join Tecumseh's war because the Choctaw had always had peaceful relations with the United States.

Student Response:

7. Student answers will vary.

Chickasaw:
Multiple Choice:

   1)   A
   2)   C
   3)   B
   4)   D
   5)   B

Guided Reading:

   1)   thousands
   2)   important
   3)   permission
   4)   accustomed
   5)   49,000

Vocabulary:

   6)   C
   7)   E
   8)   D
   9)   B
   10)   A

Correct the Statement:

   11)   Tennessee
   12)   1600s
   13)   Nanih Waiya
   14)   Sophisticated
   15)   White

Summarize:

1. Hernando de Soto became the first European to encounter the Chickasaw.
2. The Chickasaw were given $3 million for their lands.
3. Nanih Waiya was constructed in 300.
4. The Chickasaw once lived in Mississippi, Alabama, and Tennessee.
5. The Chickasaw attacked the Spaniards because they had many disagreements.
6. Stories were passed down amongst the Chickasaw orally.

Student Response:

7) Student answers will vary.

Creek:
Multiple Choice:

  1) C
  2) D
  3) A
  4) B
  5) D

Vocabulary:

  6) B
  7) D
  8) A
  9) C
  10) E

Guided Reading:

  1) Creek
  2) Language
  3) Animals
  4) Religious
  5) Nation

Correct the Statement:

  6) Hernando de Soto
  7) Mico
  8) Roots
  9) South
  10) White

Summarize:

1. The mico, or village chief, was responsible for representing the village in negotiations.
2. Yahola was another term for medicine man.
3. The Creek Nation signed several removal treaties in the 1830s.
4. The Red Sticks were eventually crushed at the Battle of Horseshoe Bend.
5. The black drink was only used during purification ceremonies because it causes vomiting.
6. These people served the mico by acting as advisers.

Student Response:

7. Student answers will vary.

Seminole:
Multiple Choice:

  1) D
  2) B
  3) A
  4) B
  5) C

Vocabulary:

  6) E
  7) B
  8) C
  9) A
  10) D

Guided Reading:

  1) Florida
  2) Muscogee
  3) Cherokee
  4) Friendly
  5) Three

History Word Builder:

  6) D
  7) A
  8) E
  9) C
  10) B

Summarize:

1. African slaves escaping from Georgia married into the tribe.
2. The federally recognized Seminole Nations are The Seminole Nation of Oklahoma, the Seminole Tribe of Florida, and the Miccosukee Tribe of Indians of Florida.
3. The US took possession of Florida in 1819.
4. The Seminole were located in Florida.
5. Pressure mounted because land-hungry settlers wanted the Seminole land.
6. The Seminole had friendly relations with the Spanish and the British

Student Response:

7) Student answers will vary

Five Civilized Tribes Test:

Vocabulary:

1. B
2. G
3. D
4. A
5. F
6. E
7. C
8. H

Completion:

9. Tattooed
10. Civilized
11. Confederation
12. Traditional
13. Tuskaloosa
14. Lacrosse

Completion:

15. Mississippi
16. Creation
17. Creek
18. Animals
19. Religious
20. Green Corn

Multiple Choice:

21. C
22. C
23. B
24. C
25. D
26. B
27. A
28. C
29. C
30. B
31. D
32. C
33. D
34. B
35. D
36. C
37. D
38. B
39. A
40. B

Creek Removal:
Multiple Choice:

1) D
2) A
3) C
4) C
5) A

Vocabulary:

1) C
2) A
3) E
4) D
5) B

Guided Reading:

6) Native Americans
7) Georgia
8) Government
9) Tribal
10) 3,000

History Word Builder:

11) D
12) E
13) A
14) C
15) B

Summarize:

1. General Winfield Scott was responsible.
2. Alabama was hoping to make the Creek as uncomfortable as possible.
3. The Indian Removal Act was passed in 1830.
4. The Native Americans were to be removed west of the Mississippi River, into Indian Territory.
5. William McIntosh signed the treaty because he personally was to receive a large sum of money.
6. The Creeks believed this treaty was not legitimate because McIntosh did not represent the entire tribe.

Student Response:

7. Student answers will vary.

Choctaw and Chickasaw Removal:
Multiple Choice:

1) C
2) B
3) D
4) B
5) A

Vocabulary:

6) B
7) A
8) E
9) D
10) C

Guided Reading:

1) Treaties
2) Snow
3) Flood
4) Froze
5) Indian Territory
6) 2,500
7) Mississippi
8) Livestock
9) Chickasaw
10) Choctaw

Summarize:

1. The Chickasaw purchased land from the Choctaw.
2. The Choctaw signed the Treaty of Dancing Rabbit Creek.
3. The Choctaw removal was to occur in 1831 and 1833.
4. The Choctaw and Chickasaw were removed to Indian Territory.
5. These things happened in the effort to make their lives so miserable, they would want to leave.
6. The Chickasaw were paid $3 million for their lands.

Student Response:

7. Student answers will vary.

Worcester v. Georgia:
Multiple Choice:

1) B
2) D
3) A
4) C
5) D

True & False:

6) F- Alabama
7) F- Gold
8) F- Cherokee Nation v. Georgia
9) T
10) F- Cherokee Nation

Guided Reading:

1) Georgia
2) Rights
3) Cherokee
4) John Ross
5) Domestic Dependent
6) Guardian
7) Government
8) Negotiate
9) Andrew Jackson
10) The Trail of Tears

Vocabulary Check:

1) B
2) D
3) C
4) A
5) C

Student Response:

6) Student answers will vary.

Cherokee Removal:
Multiple Choice:

1) B
2) A
3) D
4) C
5) B

Vocabulary:

6) D
7) A
8) E
9) B
10) C

Guided Reading:

1) Gold
2) Worcester v. Georgia
3) Elias Boudinot
4) Soldiers
5) Nine

History Word Builder:

6) E
7) B
8) A
9) D
10) C

Summarize:

1. John Ross was the principal chief of the Cherokee during the Indian Removal process.
2. Cherokee homes were burned and livestock was seized during the removal process.
3. The Treaty of New Echota was signed in 1835.
4. The Cherokee lived in Georgia, Alabama, Tennessee, and North & South Carolina.
5. White in Georgia resented the Cherokee because they were so well-off.
6. Most Cherokee refused to leave and continued struggling for their land.

Student Response:

7. Student answers will vary.

Seminole Removal:
Multiple Choice:

1) D
2) A
3) A
4) A
5) C

Vocabulary:

6) D
7) B
8) E
9) C
10) A

Guided Reading:

1) weapons
2) blood
3) alligators
4) Wildcat
5) protect

Correct the Statement:

6) Payne's
7) Thompson
8) Seminole
9) 1,500
10) Florida State

Summarize:

1. General Thomas Jesup was sent to Florida to capture Osceola.
2. The treaty stated that the Seminole would give up their tribal lands in Florida, in exchange for land in Indian Territory.
3. Osceola died on January 30, 1838.
4. The Seminole lived in Florida (or the Florida Everglades).
5. Mosquitoes were so dangerous because they spread malaria.
6. Osceola has had songs written about him, and his life has been portrayed in more than one movie.

Student Response:

7) Student answers will vary

Indian Removal Test:

Vocabulary:

1. D
2. A
3. G
4. H
5. C
6. E
7. F
8. B

Completion:

9. Native Americans
10. Treaties
11. Chickasaw
12. Gold
13. Worcester v. Georgia
14. Elias Boudinot
15. Trail of Tears
16. Osceola
17. Alligators
18. Wildcat

Multiple Choice:

19. D
20. B
21. A
22. C
23. B
24. A
25. D
26. A
27. C
28. D
29. C
30. A
31. B
32. A
33. D
34. D
35. C
36. B
37. A
38. D
39. A
40. A

Major Ridge & Elias Boudinot:
Multiple Choice:

1) C
2) B
3) D
4) D
5) A

Vocabulary:

6) B
7) E
8) A
9) D
10) C

Guided Reading:

1) Tennessee
2) communicate
3) government
4) New Echota
5) Buck Watie
6) Cherokee
7) Indian Removal Act
8) resign
9) hostility
10) retribution

Summarize:

1. Stand Watie signed the treaty but managed to survive.
2. Most of those who signed the treaty were murdered.
3. The Treaty of New Echota was signed on December 29, 1835.
4. Major Ridge settled at Honey Creek, fifty miles away from other Cherokee settlements.
5. Boudinot believed that removal was inevitable, and that they should move peacefully, before they were forced to move against their will.
6. Boudinot used his position as the editor of the Cherokee Phoenix to spread his viewpoint.

Student Response:

7. Student answers will vary.

Sequoyah:
Multiple Choice:

1) D
2) C
3) B
4) A
5) B

Vocabulary:

6) C
7) A
8) E
9) B
10) D

Guided Reading:

1) George Guess
2) War of 1812
3) popular
4) written
5) witchcraft
6) 86 characters
7) Alphabet
8) Cherokee Phoenix
9) Indian Territory
10) migrated

Summarize:

1. Sequoyah first taught his daughter to use the syllabary.
2. The Cherokee newspaper was known as the Cherokee Phoenix.
3. The Cherokee Nation adopted Sequoyah's syllabary in 1825.
4. Sequoyah was buried somewhere around the border between Mexico and Texas.
5. Sequoyah's statue was significant because he was the first Native American honored with such a statue.
6. Sequoyah spent more than a year creating his syllabary.

Student Response:

7. Student answers will vary.

John Ross:
Multiple Choice:

1) A
2) C
3) D
4) B
5) C

Guided Reading:

1) Guwisguwi
2) Cherokee
3) Horseshoe Bend
4) Chattanooga
5) Wealthiest
6) Negotiate
7) U.S. Congress
8) Major Ridge
9) Confederacy
10) 38 years

Vocabulary:

11) B
12) D
13) E
14) A
15) C

Summarize:

1. Elias Boudinot signed the treaty along with Major Ridge.
2. John Ross was elected principal chief of the Cherokee in 1828.
3. John Ross died in 1866.
4. Ross traveled to Washington DC in 1824.
5. The Creek had allied themselves with Great Britain during the War of 1812.
6. Ross own a plantation, and a river ferry.

Student Response:

7) Student answers will vary.

©Reading Through History

Stand Watie:
Multiple Choice:

1) C
2) A
3) D
4) C
5) B

Vocabulary:

6) C
7) B
8) E
9) D
10) A

Guided Reading:

1) Cherokee Nation
2) New Echota
3) lives
4) Colonel
5) Pea Ridge
6) Uniforms
7) Personally
8) Jefferson Davis
9) Hit-and-run
10) fortune

Summarize:

1. Elias Boudinot was Stand Watie's brother.
2. The book written by Harold Keith was Rifles for Watie.
3. Stand Watie surrendered on June 23, 1865.
4. Stand Watie was buried in Talequah, Oklahoma.
5. They lost their lives because they signed the treaty of New Echota.
6. His men loved him because they believed he genuinely cared about them.

Student Response:

7. Student answers will vary.

Cherokee Leaders Test:

Vocabulary:

1. E
2. A
3. B
4. D
5. C
6. F

Multiple Choice:

7. B
8. D
9. D
10. A
11. A
12. D
13. B
14. A
15. B
16. A
17. C
18. D
19. B
20. C
21. C
22. D
23. C
24. A
25. D
26. B

Completion:

27. New Echota
28. Cherokee
29. George Guess
30. War of 1812
31. Witchcraft
32. 86 characters
33. Indian Territory

Completion:

34. Horseshoe Bend
35. Chattanooga
36. Wealthiest
37. Confederacy
38. Principal Chief
39. Pea Ridge
40. Brigadier General

The Civil War in Indian Territory:
Multiple Choice:

1) C
2) C
3) A
4) C
5) D

Vocabulary:

1) A
2) D
3) B
4) C
5) E

Guided Reading:

6) recruit
7) Confederacy
8) Washita
9) suspicious
10) Round Mountain

Correct the Statement:

11) Missouri
12) Kansas
13) Union
14) Food
15) 1865

Summarize:

1. Opothleyahola was the Creek leader that established a neutral camp.
2. The Confederate victory at the Battle of Wilson's Creek convinced the Cherokee to join the Confederacy.
3. The Battle of Honey Springs occurred on August 26, 1863.
4. Most of Quantrill's raids took place in Missouri and Kansas.
5. The Battle of Cabin Creek is said to be significant because it was the first time during the Civil War that African American, white, and Native American soldiers fought alongside each other.
6. Indian Territory was devastated by the war. Thousands were dead, and homes and fields had been destroyed.

Student Response:

7. Student answers will vary.

Geronimo:
Multiple Choice:

1) D
2) A
3) C
4) B
5) A

Vocabulary:

6) A
7) C
8) E
9) B
10) D

Guided Reading:

1) Western
2) Apache
3) Cochise
4) terrified
5) 50 cents

Correct the Statement:

6) Mexican
7) Spanish
8) Mexicans
9) Southwest
10) 101 Ranch

Summarize:

1. Geronimo appeared in Theodore Roosevelt's inaugural parade.
2. Geronimo's real name was Goyathlay.
3. Geronimo surrendered for the final time in September of 1886.
4. Geronimo lived out his remaining days at Fort Sill.
5. Geronimo began his war because his family was attacked, and his mother, young wife, and three children were killed.
6. Geronimo died from pneumonia at the age of 80.

Student Response:

7. Student answers will vary.

Black Kettle:
Multiple Choice:

1) B
2) C
3) A
4) D
5) C

Guided Reading:

1) Colorado
2) Peaceful
3) Reservation
4) Lean Bear
5) Sand Creek
6) American flag
7) Warlike
8) Violent
9) Surrendered
10) Cheyenne

Vocabulary:

11) B
12) A
13) E
14) D
15) C

Summarize:

1. Colonel John Chivington was sent to the Sand Creek encampment.
2. He was told that as long as he flew that flag, no harm would come to his people.
3. The Washita Massacre occurred on November 27, 1868.
4. Gold was discovered at Pike's Peak in Colorado.
5. They had to keep moving further west to do their hunting, because of the encroaching settlers.
6. Black Kettle is remembered today as a peace maker who longed to protect his people.

Student Response:

7) Student answers will vary.

Roman Nose:
Multiple Choice:

1) C
2) B
3) A
4) D
5) C

Vocabulary:

6) E
7) B
8) D
9) C
10) A

Guided Reading:

1) Expansion
2) Cheyenne
3) Dog Soldiers
4) Fort Hays
5) War cries

Correct the Statement:

6) combat
7) Black Kettle
8) Beecher Island
9) Warriors
10) Central

Summarize:

1. Black Kettle was signing the treaties.
2. Roman Nose hoped to evict the white man from his territory, and keep his land free of fences, houses, and railroads.
3. The Battle of Beecher Island took place on September 17, 1868.
4. Roman Nose died at Beecher Island (or the Battle of Beecher Island).
5. The attacking war party was demolished so quickly because the soldiers were using seven-shot repeating rifles.
6. The U.S. military mistakenly thought Roman Nose was the principal chief of all the Cheyenne.

Student Response:

7. Student answers will vary.

General Philip Sheridan & Quanah Parker:
Multiple Choice:

1) C
2) A
3) B
4) D
5) A

Vocabulary:

1) B
2) E
3) D
4) C
5) A

Guided Reading:

6) Courage
7) Winter
8) Great Plains
9) Quanah Parker
10) Quahada
11) Texas
12) Red River
13) Horses
14) Oklahoma
15) Fort Sill

Summarize:

1. General Philip Sheridan was in charge of pacifying the Plains Indians.
2. Quanah Parker served as the principal chief of the Comanche.
3. The Red River War began in 1874.
4. General Sheridan distinguished himself at the Battles of Murfreesboro and Chattanooga.
5. The buffalo hunting bothered them because the buffalo had always been an important source of food, fuel, clothing, and construction materials for the Comanche.
6. General Sheridan established several forts including Fort Reno, Fort Arbuckle, and Fort Sill.

Student Response:

7) Student answers will vary

The Civil War & Post-War Indian Removal Test:

Vocabulary:

1. F
2. E
3. H
4. B
5. D
6. G
7. C
8. A

Multiple Choice:

9. C
10. C
11. A
12. B
13. C
14. D
15. D
16. A
17. B
18. A
19. B
20. C
21. A
22. D
23. C
24. D
25. C
26. A
27. C
28. D
29. B
30. D

Completion:

31. Confederacy
32. Apache
33. Geronimo
34. Colorado
35. Reservation
36. Sand Creek
37. American Flag
38. War-like
39. Dog Soldiers
40. Quanah Parker

©Reading Through History

Chisholm Trail:
Multiple Choice:

1) C
2) A
3) B
4) D
5) B

Vocabulary:

6) E
7) A
8) D
9) B
10) C

Guided Reading:

1) fourteen
2) eastern
3) cold
4) 10 cents
5) Kansas City

Correct the Statement:

6) Red River
7) Civil War
8) Spring or Fall
9) A dollar
10) El Reno

Summarize:

1. The trail was named after Jesse Chisholm.
2. The best estimates range from 1.5 million up to 5 million.
3. The trail became popular with ranchers after the Civil War.
4. The drives ended at Abilene, Kansas.
5. The cattle were dangerous because stampedes were a constant threat.
6. Jesse Chisholm helped the government negotiate with different tribes.

Student Response:

7. Student answers will vary.

Belle Starr:
Multiple Choice:

1) A
2) C
3) B
4) B
5) D

Vocabulary:

6) E
7) D
8) A
9) C
10) B

Guided Reading:

1) Guns
2) Raiders
3) Rustling
4) $30,000
5) Robber's Roost
6) Jesse James
7) Horse theft
8) Cherokee
9) Fiction
10) Porum

Summarize:

1. Tom Watson shot Belle Starr.
2. Horse theft was the only crime she was ever charged with or convicted of.
3. Belle Starr died in 1889.
4. Robber's Cave State Park is just outside Wilburton, Oklahoma.
5. Watson was furious at Belle because she turned him away and refused to harbor him.
6. Belle committed most of her criminal activities dressed as a man.

Student Response:

7. Student answers will vary.

David Payne &The Boomer Movement:
Multiple Choice:

1) C
2) A
3) D
4) D
5) B

Vocabulary:

6) D
7) E
8) C
9) B
10) A

Guided Reading:

1) Two million
2) promoters
3) Unassigned Lands
4) Colonies
5) U.S. Army

Correct the Statement:

6) Non-Native Americans
7) Son
8) Valuable
9) Kansas
10) Thousands

Summarize:

1. David Payne was the leader of the Boomer Movement.
2. The Oklahoma War Chief was the title of the newspaper.
3. E.C. Boudinot's article appeared on February 17, 1879.
4. The colonies started to form in Arkansas City, Caldwell, and Hunnewell, Kansas.
5. The farmers were desperate for their own piece of land.
6. Payne had spent much time in southern Kansas and explored much of current-day Oklahoma.

Student Response:

7) Student answers will vary.

The Land Run:
Multiple Choice:

1) B
2) D
3) C
4) A
5) B

Vocabulary:

6) B
7) D
8) E
9) C
10) A

Guided Reading:

1) Boomers
2) Land give away
3) soldiers
4) noon
5) 100,000

History Word Builder:

6) C
7) B
8) E
9) A
10) D

Summarize:

1. President Benjamin Harrison issued the proclamation.
2. These people stared general stores, lumber stores, and stage coach businesses.
3. The first land run occurred on April 22, 1889.
4. The biggest and most spectacular land run occurred in the Cherokee Outlet.
5. It was often difficult to tell who claimed the land first.
6. They were describing it as "the garden spot of the world".

Student Response:

7. Student answers will vary.

Life on the Prairie:
Multiple Choice:

1) C
2) B
3) C
4) A
5) C

Vocabulary:

6) A
7) C
8) E
9) D
10) B

Guided Reading:

1) tent
2) thick
3) maintenance
4) plowed
5) bartering
6) eggs
7) fuel
8) homes
9) clothing
10) succeed

Summarize:

1. Settlers would often barter with the neighbors.
2. Sod homes were made of long strips of dirt.
3. A family might go on such an expedition right before winter.
4. The neighbors might be miles away on the frontier.
5. It was difficult to plow the fields because the prairie grasses had deep roots.
6. A sod house usually had one or two rooms.

Student Response:

7. Student answers will vary

Statehood:
Multiple Choice:

1) A
2) B
3) D
4) D
5) A

Vocabulary:

6) E
7) A
8) D
9) C
10) B

Guided Reading:

1) Tribal
2) Oklahoma
3) Lincoln
4) Sequoyah
5) U.S. Congress

Correct the Statement:

6) Oklahoma
7) Indian
8) Late 1800s
9) Different
10) Kansas

Summarize:

1. The Native American state was going to be named Sequoyah.
2. The goal of the Dawes Allotment Act was to stimulate the assimilation of Native Americans into mainstream American culture.
3. The name Oklahoma was officially approved in 1890.
4. The western half of the state was known as Oklahoma Territory.
5. The two territories had developed different ways of life, and came from very different heritages.
6. Oklahoma Territory grew as the various native tribes negotiated with the government, and then those lands were given away to settlers through land runs.

Student Response:

7) Student answers will vary

The Oklahoma State Constitutional Convention:
Multiple Choice:

1) B
2) B
3) D
4) B
5) A

Vocabulary:

6) E
7) A
8) D
9) B
10) C

Guided Reading:

1) Enabling
2) 55
3) Farmers
4) Democrats
5) Charles Haskell
6) Alcohol
7) William Jennings Bryan
8) September
9) 1958
10) 46th

Summarize:

1. William H. Murray was the president.
2. The Sequoyah Convention laid much of the foundation for the Oklahoma state constitution.
3. Roosevelt signed the proclamation on November 16, 1907.
4. The public announcement was made in Guthrie, Oklahoma.
5. There are many progressive measures because the constitution was written during the Progressive Movement.
6. The people were allowed to vote on the issue of prohibition.

Student Response:

7) Student answers will vary

Boomers, the Land Run & Statehood Test:

Vocabulary:

1. F
2. C
3. A
4. B
5. H
6. G
7. D
8. E

Vocabulary:

9. D
10. G
11. E
12. B
13. H
14. F
15. C
16. A

Multiple Choice:

17. B
18. A
19. A
20. B
21. B
22. B
23. D
24. C
25. D
26. A
27. D
28. D
29. B
30. B
31. D
32. C
33. B
34. C
35. B
36. C
37. A
38. B
39. D
40. C
41. A
42. B

Completion:

43. Unassigned Lands
44. Noon
45. 100,000
46. Bartering
47. Sequoyah
48. Enabling
49. Democrats
50. 46th

Early History to Statehood Post-Assessment:
Multiple Choice:

1. B
2. A
3. A
4. A
5. C
6. D
7. B
8. B
9. A
10. D
11. B
12. D
13. C
14. C
15. C
16. B
17. C
18. C
19. D
20. D
21. B
22. A
23. D
24. B
25. C
26. D
27. A
28. C
29. D
30. C
31. D
32. D
33. C
34. B
35. D
36. B
37. B
38. D
39. B
40. C
41. A
42. B
43. C
44. C
45. A
46. C
47. D
48. B
49. C
50. A
51. C
52. C
53. A
54. D
55. D
56. B
57. A
58. A
59. B
60. D
61. A
62. D
63. B
64. B
65. C

Multiple Choice (continued):

66. C
67. B
68. C
69. B
70. C
71. A
72. B
73. C
74. A
75. B

Made in the USA
Coppell, TX
25 June 2024

33905760R00111